Success with Apples and Pears to Eat and Drink

A practical gardeners' guide to varieties, husbandry, harvesting, storing and making juices, cyder and perry.

se Apple Mill

D1368943

Published by
Groundnut Publishing

SUCCESS WITH APPLES AND PEARS
TO EAT AND DRINK

First published in 2002 by
Groundnut Publishing, Vinces Road, Diss, Norfolk IP22 4HG

Text: Alan Rowe

Editor: Ernest List
Drawings: Alan Rowe & Sheila Wright
Photography: Ernest List & Alan Rowe

Printed in Great Britain by Eye Press Ltd, Diss, Norfolk.

ISBN 0-9527141-3-2

Cover Photograph: Kidd's Orange Red and Josephine de Malines

CONTENTS

Foreword

Introduction

FOREWORD

We live in a unique time when all things are available to those who can afford them. A time of Global trade on a never before heard of scale, when planes can circle the world to bring us whichever luxury we desire, whenever we want, and from wherever. But in buying into Globalisation we are in danger of losing sight of one of our greatest luxuries, that of savouring good tastes and appreciating excellent quality.

Apples have been in the service of man since he first learnt to walk and reach up to pick. This book reminds us of their enduring importance, not just as a food and a luxury but also in symbolism, religion and legends. The significance of apples and pears is traced through the history of Western civilisation, the domestication and perfection of the cherished fruit advancing with each through the centuries. Now, after some 7,000 years of cultivation, we are in a position of some responsibility to retain the apple's status and uphold its standards at a time when its esteem is at a low ebb.

Alan Rowe's enthusiasm in a search for excellence goes a long way to inspiring us to do our bit to rediscover the special tastes, to delight in the aromas and textures of 'quality' fruit by motivating us towards collecting and growing some of the best cultivars available for our own gustatory delights. There is nothing more enjoyable for the hunter-gatherer in each of us than to pick our own fruit and munch it then and there, or make something pleasant from it to eat or drink. The simple instructions are all here, from choosing, planting and caring for trees to the pleasurable creation of cider, or cyder Suffolk-style, and perry.

As one who has had a long association with cider apples and appreciate their distinctiveness, I am intrigued to learn of their origins and ancestors. Those of us who find shop shelves stocked with indifferent and bland beverages will be delighted to read about real cyder made in the time-honoured way. The supermarket produce is not for discerning palates. Perhaps there is already a glimmer of hope for the future, for quality traditional cider is making a come-back, superior sorts of apples and pears are once more cherished and orchards are being lovingly restored. Read this book and be inspired to appreciate the differences and encourage the renaissance.

LIZ COPAS
Cider Pomologist
Long Ashton Research Station, Bristol
July 2002

We are witnessing the continuing collapse of the English orchard industry. The last 25 years have seen Suffolk's orchards reduced by 90% and the land used to 'grow' houses. The rest of East Anglia, The Southeast, The Southwest and The Midlands are in much the same state. Home fruit growing, agriculture and horticulture become little more than pretty, thematic, backdrops for the tourist industry. Globalisation's 'truth' is that we can import more cheaply than we can grow and so require only 'Service industries' – land is a commodity which is to be exploited in the 'here and now', rather than as hitherto – to be passed on... Only a few weeks ago I heard an 'authority' on *Today* pronounce that *'The most unprofitable use for a meadow is to keep cows on it'*.

My opinion is, that which appears to be cheap in the short term, will be paid for eventually and dearly... I recall my grandfather repeating that *'cheap'* proved generally, to have been *'nasty'* and that *'only nothing comes for nothing!'*

There is no nationally driven will to prevent the decline of home-grown produce and even if such will evolves, it may come too late.

Fruit genebanks exist only through the endeavours of organisations such as The Brogdale Trust and The Royal Horticultural Society and in our kitchen gardens. The principal retailers in the United Kingdom offer only a dozen or so of the thousands of apple varieties and far fewer of the hundreds of pear cultivars. Most of those, which are offered, are imported and have been chosen for their cropping potentials, their long shelf life, their eye-appeal and their tolerance of up to 12,000 miles of transporting. They do not, necessarily, have qualities to excite the palate – obviously none of those which come from remaining on the tree until optimum picking times and finishing perfection in store.

There can be no doubt that the very best apples and pears are those which are home-grown and where could be more home grown than in your own kitchen garden?

In the introduction to ' The History and Virtues of Cyder, which was published in 1982, R. K. French asserts, *"Cyder is no longer made"* and he dismisses modern offerings as, *"Bland, pasteurised, diluted, carbon dioxide injected cider – a beverage"*. "Cyder", he says, *"is a living wine with subtlety"*. And continues, *"to hope that after more than a century of reputation collapse, it is surely time for the rebirth of 'The Cyderist'"*. He was referring to sickly, saccharin sweet, commercial ciders – little more than apple flavoured soft drinks... And he was correct... It <u>was</u> time for cyder's return and since the eighties it has become usual for merchants to offer a number of 'Real Ciders', which I think of as 'cyders'

– as do some commercial cyderists. Unfortunately, too many 'ciders' remain – made from indeterminate varieties, imported as apple concentrates – and far too many remain of the peardrop flavoured fizzy drinks which are styled, most fancifully, as 'perry', which do nothing for home growers and nothing but harm to cyders' and perrys' reputations.

Fortunately, even when times were at their worst, wherever apples grew, there were local cyderists – making, perhaps, only enough for themselves and friends – but practising and amending methods which they had learned from a previous generation of neighbourhood cyderists. There are more cyderists now than there were 20 years ago.

I began making cyder in the latter part of the '50s when the family settled in Suffolk to find mature Worcester, James Grieve, Allington Pippin, Laxton Superb, Codlin, Lord Derby and Bramley apples and Laxton Superb pears already on our land. It was Joe 'Dusty' Miller, the Mendlesham cyderist, who taught me how to make cyder in the East Anglian fashion and I hope to pass on a version of that skill. This book outlines something of the story of apples and pears and their close association with Mankind over thousands of years. I trust that it will prove of use to kitchen gardeners as a handbook for the cultivation and for other enjoyments of apples and pears.

ALAN ROWE
April 2002

'Don't it always seem to go, that you don't know what you've got – 'til it's gone?'
(Joni Mitchell, Folk Singer)

Old Devonshire Drinking Song

I were brought up on cyder and I be a hundred and two.
But tha' be nothin' when you come to think.
My father and mother be still in the pink.
And they was brought up on cyder – Of the rare old Tavistock brew.
And me granfer drink quarts, for he's one o' the sports –
As was brought up on cyder too!

This book is dedicated to Joseph Wilgress 'Dusty' Miller of Mendlesham. Wheelwright, Carpenter, General Faker and Cydermaker *(1875-1962)*

and with sincere thanks to...

My wife Anne for editorial comment and indexing.

Liz Copas of IACR Long Ashton for information, Sweet Coppin photograph and proof reading.

Henry Chevallier-Guild of The Aspall Cyder House, Debenham, for access to orchards, equipment and information.

Professor Laurence Smith for proof reading and editorial comment.

Howard Stringer of the RHS Fruit Group and The Brogdale Trust for editorial comment and information.

The Institute for Arable Crop Research, Long Ashton, for permission to reproduce perry pear photographs from Luckwill and Pollards' (1963) *'Perry Pears'*.

Dave Sherriff for *'1,936 Brogdale Apples'*.

Sheila Wright for rootstock and training sketches.

Alan Rowe

CHAPTER ONE

From Pangaea to the Global Market

Flowering Plants and Origins

Flowering plants, the **Angiospermae**, came to be during Cretaceous times – sometime between one hundred and twenty and eighty million years ago.

It is believed that in the beginning, was the **'Ancestral Complex'** from which sprang the various degrees of specialisation. The superorder **Rosidae** 'The Rose superfamily', was one of the earliest to emerge. It is complex and is one of the many battlegrounds enjoyed by botanists, where 'lumpers' and 'splitters' seek to promote or demote families, genera and species… is *Pyrus*, the pear, no more than a subspecies of Malus, the apple, or does it stand alone? Should **Maloideae** be elevated to 'Family' status or left where it is?… And so on… and so on.

Within **Rosidae** lie peas, proteas, houseleeks, pomegranates, dogwoods, spurges, hollies, carrots, geraniums and many others, which are dissimilar to the untutored eye. Here, too, is included the order **Rosales** which includes the family **Rosaceae** which contains the subfamily **Maloideae**. This subfamily includes *Malus* 'The Apple' which was the result of a most unlikely primeval pairing – a Spirea (Chromosome number 8) mated with a Plum (Chromosome number 9) and an entirely new and unique form of fruit – The Pome (Chromosome number 17) – had 'happened'. This primal Pome, laden with prussic acid, for its defence, became today's apples, pears and medlars, quinces and hawthorns.

This germinal crossing took place when the World had but one continent, now styled **Pangaea**. When Pangaea fragmented into continental plates, each carried its piece of the Rose gene pool to develop in continentally differing ways.

That which we call Eurasia had the wherewithal for **Maloideae** – in particular in and around Turkmenistan, Uzbekistan and Khirgizia and in the Tien Shan – 'The Heavenly Mountains'. It is as certain as can be that the primary ancestor of every *Malus domestica* – the domestic apple – was *Malus sierversii*, which is native to Khirgizia.

Here, vast apple, pear, peach and plum forest dressed with grapevines once stretched from the Caspian Sea to the Tien Shan and most especially in Alma Ata (Father of Apples)…

This Garden of Eden straddles the Old Silk Road and all our modern dessert, culinary and cyder apples have happened, or have been bred from progeny of the seed of apples dropped or traded by merchants and migrants as they travelled or settled along this ancient commercial highway.

Other species which have given the domestic apple its diversity are the long keeping, but bitter, Caucasian M.*orientalis*, the cold resistant Siberian crab M.*baccata*, the astringent Turkish crab M.*sylvestris*, the small but very hardy Manchurian crab M.*mandshurica* and the larger Chinese crab M.*prunifolia.* It is where these species overlap and share bounds with already arrived hybrids that the seemingly infinite new forms have arisen. There is no other fruit on earth, which has such infinite variety of form, texture, colour and complexities of flavour and scent.

Modern research suggests that no more than 30% of the genetic variance resting in the forests of Alma-Ata has made its way into the world's domestic varieties. There are forms there, which show every attribute of the domestic apple and many more, which are absent. There are forms, which are resistant to its ailments and to its pests and which, naturally, have never known 'sprays'.

Some root with ease, when a 'mother apple' can cover large areas with both suckers and progeny. Every pip is, potentially, a new variety and a future parent.

It is greatly to the misfortune of our descendants that they will not have the opportunity to study, wholly, the Alma-Ata genepool. Much of it went when large areas of forest was clear-felled to make way for Soviet Aparatchics' dachas and still more is going to make way for the dachas of Capitalist Russia's New Rich… Without doubt this is an unconscionable destruction of Paradise – But we do well to remember that most of Britain's native forest were 'developed' long ago…

The codifying of living things is a matter of setting… From the superorder, which includes things with generally similar attributes, to degrees of speciality in families, genus, species and cultivars.

Cyderapples are considered to be of sufficient similarity to domestic apples to be included as M.*domesticus*, but research at Cornell University (circa 1997) suggests otherwise.

In attempting to establish apple pedigrees Cornell pomologists created a genealogical map which included family 'markers'. Sixty-five of the sixty-six varieties which were tested, fell within the markers and so were seen to be closely related to M.*sierversii*, but the cyder variety 'Chisel Jersey' shared the fewest of the commonly held genes. It seemed to be closer to the crabs M.*sylvestris* and M.*pumila*, both of which are native to Europe and originated in Asia Minor. The presently held view is that whilst cyderapples began their journey in Khirgizia, much of their genepool was established during a long stay in Asia Minor.

Cyder, desert, crab and culinary varieties are most willing to cross-pollinate, to the extent that it is often difficult to differentiate 'wild' from 'cultivated'… except that true crabs have no down on their new growth.

It is most surprising that such a sexually indiscriminate genus refuses to mate with other pomes. Linnaeus (1707-78) considered it to be no more than a subgenus of *Pyrus* (The pear) but, singularly amongst the pomes, it will not accept any other as a natural partner, whether by sexual union or as a stock or scion.

Pear, Quince, Medlar and Hawthorn

The pear *Pyrus*, the Quince *Cydonia*, the Medlar *Mespilus* and the Hawthorn *Crataegus*, are descendants of the primal Pangean Pome, but, unlike the apple, pears and quinces and medlars and hawthorns are quite tolerant of their relatives. It is, for instance, usual practice to graft pears onto quince stocks in order to encourage precocious fruiting and Medlar may be grafted onto quince or hawthorn.

The pear may be grouped as 'European' (Dessert), 'Warden' (Culinary), 'Perry' (Latin *pirus* pear, Old English *pirige* and *peru*) and 'Asian'.

Both dessert and culinary pears are considered as descended from the native mainland European pears *Pyrus communis* and *P.nivalis*, having been hybridised naturally and with Man's intervention, with other species and hybrid pears.

The culinary pear is gritty and hard and requires long stewing or baking to become pleasantly edible… a neighbour said of the fruit from an ancient 'I-ron' pear, which used to stand in 'Burnt Cottage Meadow' next to us… *"Do you put him in your Rayburn for a couple of days – Then do you throw him away!"* It was, most certainly, of I-ron! Hindsight suggests that we should have waited longer before trying to use it – for it would not have been allowed to live for so long without usefulness. My sons used to take the small fruit, straight from the tree, chew all the flavour away and then spit out the gritty pulp. When the cattle went during the 1980's, as did the meadow and its mushrooms, so did the last vestige of the cottage, which had burnt down sometime before the 1884 Ordinance Survey and that of its kitchen garden. These cooking pears, known alternatively as Wardens, perhaps after 16th Century Bedfordshire Warden Abbey Pear and here in Suffolk as 'I-ron' pears, will keep until the following May. Some have more sweetness than others, do, all are gritty but are usually superior to unripe dessert pears for cooking.

The truly 'dessert' pear is a latecomer and began with 17th and 18th Century French hybrids. The perrypear is descended from the European species *P.communis* and *P.nivalis*. All perry pears are very tannic and are totally inedible raw, but can be eaten cooked. They have a gritty 'stone' ring around the pip cavity. The Asian pear is derived from the East Asian species *P.ussuriensis* and *P.serotina*. Its cultivars are usually russeted and apple-shaped. They lack in flavour and scent when compared with European dessert pears, especially if they have been grown in the UK. They are sometimes offered in supermarkets and are said to improve salads.

Man Myth and the last few thousand years

Wanderers

Manlike creatures evolved to be something like us by about four hundred thousand years ago. That is to say, that for about three hundred and ninety-nine million and six hundred thousand years after Creation's Big Bang, the Earth was without creatures like us.

Hunter-gatherer-fishermen walked here from what are now Africa, Portugal, Spain and France. They are unlikely to have found apples or pears but would have eaten azaroles and other hawthorn-like pomes. Others walked from 'Denmark' and the east and would have known apples and pears.

By around 2,000BC they had become the megalith builders of Callanish and Stonehenge and a thousand years later they had become influenced by the westward advance of Indo-Aryan-Kelt farming and fruit-farming. Sometime before 10,000BC, when much of the great southern and northern ice sheets melted, the Atlantic broke through the Afro-Eurasian landbridges to flood the Mediterranean and the Black Sea basins and our landbridges with Europe were swamped.

Sumer

There is much evidence of there being settlements more than 7,000 years ago, for example in Jordan, Formosa and Malta, but our first historical evidence of 'Civilisation' comes from the Tigris-Euphrates Sumerians of around 4000BC and they referred to there having been 'Civilisation' long before they had become literate.

Their contribution to all civilisations, which have followed, was immense. The Creation, The Flood, The Tree of Knowledge, Forbidden Fruit, The Fall from immortality and their interpretation of Nature is saved on thousands of clay tablets of cuneiform script. The Sumerians organised agriculture, horticulture, town planning and libraries. They discovered fermentation and found that wine could make bad water safe. They made vineyards and orchards, enclosed fields and had town gardens, for pleasure and recreation.

Every time we measure an angle or describe a circle we use their visualisation of 360° and we use their Base-60 arithmetic whenever we tell the time. They knew of the 3, 4, 5 right-angled triangle, they were civil engineers and piped water and made irrigation systems. They had standard weights and measures, stored grain and preserved meat. They minted coins to <u>facilitate</u> barter, but maintained relative values, to be carried in the head. *Thousands of years on – in fact, last harvest – an East Anglian Apple-grower, who had had to leave his fruit unharvested, said that he and his father before him, had reckoned on a pound of apples being worth a pint of beer. 'But beer is now £2 a pint and I can't get 50p a pound for apples!'… It is just not sensible for beer to have become <u>worth</u> such a differential, any more than some branded bottled waters can be <u>worth</u> three or four times as much as petrol… Is it that our ability to equate relative values by experience, has been erased by such as 'What the market will stand' and '50% Free?'*

They invented commerce and bureaucracy and their King-priests' knowledge enabled them to forecast dates for solstices and equinoxes and so direct the times for sowing and harvest and exercise civilising control. They codified law and assigned civilised values to conduct. They coined and observed that behaviour which is essential in a sustainable society… *'Do unto others as you would have them to do unto you.'*

The Gilgamesh Epic records how the 'two thirds' divine Gilgamesh slew 'The Guardian of the Forest' (*The Green Man*), who stood between him and 'The Fruit of the Tree of Knowledge', which would complete his immortality and he spurned Ishtar's lust for him. Scorned, The Goddess of Love and War sent a Serpent to snatch the fruit from him and to swallow it… Thus King Gilgamesh lived only the span of a sub-god, but the serpent lived forever, by shedding skins.

Late in 2001, the Sumerian reference to previous civilisations was confirmed when the ruins of a large city were sighted beneath The Arabian Gulf.

Harrapa

This contemporary of, or later than Sumer, Indus valley civilisation, shared similar deities and myths, but portrayed the Sumerian God and his creation as *Manu* (*Sanskrit* Man) a hermaphrodite and believed that Manu degenerated later to become the two sexes… Much later The Holy Bible speaks of *making man in his own image* and of *Sons of God* but *Daughters of Man.*

The Ancient Egyptians' climate denied them the cultivation of apples, but they held them to be 'Food of the Gods' and it is recorded that King Rhamses II had his great liking for them satisfied 'from the north'.

Romano-Graeco-Judaic Cultures and 'The Apple'

By 1500BC the Aryan speaking Indo-Europeans began migrating from the north of the Himalayas and by around 1000BC they were established, in Northern India and all around the Mediterranean basin. Israel was a Nation. In 1100BC Tilgath the Assyrian had taken Babylon and by 900BC the Greeks had colonies from Asia Minor to Southern Italy. Sargon the First, Emperor of Akkadia-Sumer had been dead for as long as Constantine the Great has been for us.

The Ancient Greeks

The Greek Pantheon, had major Gods, including – Apollo The Sun God and 'Guardian of Apples', Gaia, Mother Earth *Who Eats Her Children'* and Aphrodite 'Goddess of Love and War' – and hundreds more gods, demi-gods, nymphs and lesser immortals.

The Gods required annual renewal by eating Golden Apples from the Tree of Knowledge, tended by the Three Nymphs of the Hesperides (*Probably 'The Azores'*). The tree was always under attack from The Titans, who had been cast from Olympus. (*It was one the Titans, Prometheus, who stole Fire from Apollo and gave it to Mankind.*)

That the apple was so wondrous came from observation… If it was cut in half along the stem, the apple had obvious fertility symbolism. If cut across the stem its seeds were in the form of 'The pentagon' which had, uniquely, the same number of diagonals as it had sides. These diagonals created a smaller pentagon within and the process could be repeated beyond Man's vision, to an 'atomic' combination of Fire, Air, Water and Earth (Empodocles circa 485BC; *a-tomos* to cut). The apple's 'pentagon' was created from larger, invisible pentagons, which contained the heavens and *ad infinitum*.

If a farmer sowed *Emmer* grain, then he reaped an *Emmer* harvest, but… If he sowed seed from his finest apple tree, then, many years later, he had the chagrin of harvesting from apple trees, which were all different and with few, which were as good as their dam. Clearly, *Apples were God-given and guarded jealously!*

These Gods were completely amoral and capricious. They were Proud, Envious, Wrathful, Avaricious, Lustful, Gluttonous and Slothful. But, unlike mortals, they were immune from consequence. Their gifts had, always, two faces – as had any advice given by their go-betweens The Oracles.

'...Hermes, Messenger of the Gods, tricked Paris into giving a Golden Apple – which was not his to give – to the fairest of Hera, Athene and Aphrodite – who had access to as many Golden Apples as they wanted! Hera promised power and riches, Athene promised wisdom and victories and Aphrodite promised the love of Helen of Sparta. In choosing Aphrodite, Paris won Helen... The hatred of the other two goddesses... A seven-year war and the obliteration of Troy...'

'...The Nymph Atalanta 'Fleetest of Foot' was bound to perpetual virginity, but promised herself to any man who could outrun her, safe in the knowledge that not one could. Many had tried, but had won the second prize, which was Death! Aphrodite gave Hippomenes Three Golden Apples to throw ahead of Atalanta who could not resist stopping, to retrieve them and so she was beaten and dishonoured. Hippomenes, in his lust, forgot to thank Aphrodite and was turned, quite appropriately, into a beast.'

Israelites

The Israelites, with a lasting hatred for other 'Sons of Abraham' changed Ishtar, Goddess of Love and War, into the disobedient Eve and their God Jahweh dispatched all unfavoured Angels to Hell under the leadership of Satan 'The prince of Darkness', (*Hebrew* 'The Enemy') – who was Prometheus, recycled. The Syrians 'Lord God of the Highest Heavens' *Baal-Zebub* became Beelzibub, Lord of the Flies, Satan's Lieutenant. The Harappan hermaphrodite *Manu* became the man Adam and the Tree of Knowledge of Good and Evil, which was in the Paradise of Eden (= *delight or pleasure*), had its fruit forbidden to Adam and Eve. Satan, in the shape of 'The Serpent', tempted Eve to taste of the fruit and she had no difficulty in tempting Adam. They were cast from Paradise (Persian *pairidaissa* walled garden) but it was Woman who was condemned to have responsibility for all worldly sin and to be man's vessel and vassal for thousands of years. ...Eve was *The Apple of Ishtar*, which is all sweetness on one side but gall on the other – She was *The Apple of Sodom*, beautiful to behold, but full of ashes – And at the root of all evil was a love of *Mammon*, the Syrian 'God of Worldly Riches'.

In translation through the Greek *Malum* 'Fruit of the Tree of Knowledge' becomes 'apple' and the apple's moral duality is confirmed in translation by the Latin *mal* – evil.

Romans, Kelts, Moors, Germanic tribes and Northmen

The Romans' were a practical people and their best qualities lay in being imperialist, in building and in adapting. They absorbed cultures and Gods along with conquest. They took on the Greek Pantheon, but with changed names, and did likewise with Keltic deities. Religion was seen as being of personal choice and remained so until, in its twilight, a doomed Rome turned, most cruelly, upon Christians and others for diversion.

They were excellent gardeners and hybridisers and they furthered the Greek art of grafting. The wholesale use of grafting marked a huge advance in fruit growing and made it possible to plant orchards of chosen variety. Pliny (1st Century AD) lists twenty apple varieties by qualities of taste, smell and season and Decio, a variety said to be 'Roman', remains in the Brogdale Faversham collection. Apicius's Cookery Book (1st Century AD) recommends that 'Apples cooked with coriander and honey' should be served at the end of a meal. The Romans loved dinner parties when they would serve their guests produce from their own kitchen gardens. Horace considered that all meals should begin with eggs and end with apples, with the dessert apple being reserved for the 'Second Dinner' – served in the orchard and out of the gaze of slaves – where their aphrodisiac and breath-freshening qualities would aid the usual after-dinner dalliance.

The 2nd Century Romanised-Greek Galen, hypothesised that 'All was of Air, Earth, Fire and Water and these elements were humoured by qualities of Cool, Dry, Hot and Moist. The human body he said had these elements and qualities in such as Hot/Blood and Cool/Phlegm and Dry/Black and Moist/Yellow Biles.

Cider and Perry were 'cold' and so should not precede a meal – for digestion required heat. However, they were ideal for cooling the heat resulting from work.

Galen had it that cider or perry, when taken alone, would move the liver into 'melancholy' (*Latin* black bile). There followed the production of balancing moist yellow bile, which encouraged its owner to purge the annoyance and *'flux with haste'*, for Galen's theory required that to be 'in good humour', required 'good balance.' A 'Galenic' tale comes from 18th century Somerset... The new vicar's wife was 'visiting' and on being told (not surprisingly) – that the house had no sherry, said that she would try 'this perry of yours'. 'I wouldn't Ma'am', said the labourer – 'It goo rund loyk thunder and come owt loyk loytnin!'

The Romans had many dessert, culinary and perry cultivars and much-preferred 'pearwine' to 'applewine' for, unlike cyderapples which work to dryness, many perry pears have some unfermentable sugars and finish sweeter. They are given the credit for introducing the apple to Britain. It seems much more likely to me that it arrived, either naturally in hand, or in the gut of humans, birds and animals during the previous 300,000 years, when as in the rest of Europe, some worthwhile cultivars must have occurred. The Romans were never to have control, or a real desire, for settlement over much more than 25% of the Main Island, during their 400 years occupation and virtually none over 'Scotland', 'Ireland' and 'Wales'. What is certain is that they planted their favourite cultivars in the orchards of 'Kent' and 'Sussex'. It is certain, also, that Druidic Solstic and Equinoxial ceremonies had required apples, pears and kissing-boughs and mistletoe long before Claudius had required his 'Triumph.'

The Graeco-Roman Apple-nymph *Pomona* and *Vertuminus*, 'The Harvest God' would co-exist, comfortably, with the Celts' *Samhain*, with which they shared similar rites. Cyder drinking was common to all Kelts and the British Celtic cyder tradition continues in Worcestershire, in Monmouth and in the Southwest of England.

Christianity and Islam

Rome degenerated into Western and Eastern Empires and eventually, The Two Holy Empires. These became increasingly intolerant, not only of other faiths, but each of the other. The Heathens' Gods were re-invented as Saints and Demons, devils, goblins and hobgoblins, incubi and succubi, and witches were invented to carry out the Devil's work… The Early Roman Church suppressed and vilified all other faiths and practised a greatly perverted Christianity – essentially a wholly compassionate and tolerant Faith – much as today, some psychotic Mullahs pervert Islam…

Islam arose when many Semitic peoples were lapsing into the worshipping of pre-Biblical pantheons and The Koran includes much of the Old Testament's myth and rigour. It refers to Abraham and other Old Testament persons and Christ and upholds the right of Christians and all other Faiths to own and to practise their beliefs without hindrance.

The Islamic Moors were considerably more cultured than their European contemporaries and brought Universities and scientific enquiry to Iberia and Langue D'oc together with 'Zero' – that most useful of mathematical tools.

I do not know, why or when Islam forbade the drinking of alcohol, but my untutored reading of a translation of The Koran, suggests to me that it implies discouragement, rather than makes proscription.

The Moors were fine farmers and makers of pleasure gardens and they were fruit growers and made wines and cyder until at least the end of the 8th Century. (Ibn Bassal *'The Book of Agriculture'* c.1000). Normandy cyder orchards were improved with Cantabrian and Asturian stock. Cantabria and Asturia continue the Moorish cyder tradition.

Neither Roman Christianity nor Islam did much to improve women's lot, for both regarded them as the 'Daughters of Eve' and Satan's allies. Renaissance paintings depicting an apple in Eve's hand symbolise 'Evil' – in a man's hand it is a symbol of 'Good'… And when Tannhäuser sings of, 'having given <u>his</u> apple to Venus' – as it were – his Prince compels him to make a pilgrimage to Rome to seek The Pope's forgiveness.

After the Romans left and the **Germanic Tribes** had pushed the British to the western and northern fringes and after Goths and Visigoths and Franks had adopted 'The Holy Roman Church', missionaries convinced rulers of the powerful self-advantages, which came with Christendom… Throughout Europe, Kings prayed with Rome, but crossed their fingers and touched wood, as did their subjects.

The early Church captured the solstic, the equinoxial and all other pre-Christian festivals – just as Business-Mammon is appropriating Christmas and Easter as Spending Festivals. But Folklore is difficult to erase, for it keeps its power through being passed orally from mind to mind. For examples, we can soon be reminded that…The Irish Celt hero, Blamain, was conceived for virgin birth, when his mother ate a magic apple… That Bran and other Celtic heroes carried apple branches for the renewal of their powers and that the Celt hero King Arthur is buried at Avalon *(The Isle of Apples)* and awaits the call to arms. The Celtic Samhain and Roman Pomona festivals, which were around the now All Hallows Eve, celebrated glimpses into the Underworld, as the Nature Gods made their winter retreat. Maidens put applepips beneath their pillows for dreams of true love and villagers visited friends to 'Duck or Bob for apples' and gave 'keepers' – apples stored in bran – as gifts.

In midwinter, evergreens were dressed with apples and appleskins and there were kissing boughs of holly, ivy and mistletoe to encourage the fertility, which came with the Spirits' return. Hard nuts *(Originally* 'nut' = 'fruit') were fit to eat and exchanged as gifts… *I had a little nut tree. Nothing did it bear, but a Golden Apple and a Golden Pear…* Even today, the tale persists that Gilgamesh's immortal great-grandfather is in a Khirgizistan Paradise Garden and tends The Tree of Knowledge… It produces golden apples and golden pears and other golden fruits according to whether he sings or whistles or hums… and it remains the tradition for Caucasian brides to roll under apple trees to guarantee their fecundity.

The Nordic Gods lived in Asgard and Odin was supreme. He and his Pantheon had to have their youth refreshed annually by the Golden Apples, which were grown by the maiden Iduna, or there would be no spring and all on Earth would perish. These apples grew 'in the south' on *Yggdrasil,* The Tree of Life and Knowledge and Time and Space. This evergreen Ash held apart Heaven and Earth, Night and Day and Time and Space and its symbol was a cross within The Sun's circle. It dripped honey and its roots grew about The Fountain of all Virtues.

Loki (*'luck'*) precipitated *'The War of the Gods'* when he had Balder the Bright shot in his mortal heel and so killed by a mistletoe arrow. Balder's mother had not asked the mistletoe when she had held him up by the heel and had asked the rest of Nature to protect him, *'because it was rootless and neither of the Earth nor of the Heavens'*. It was to the Earth's good fortune that Odin's alliance won and certain favoured Gods returned. 'Balder, Bright One and God of Apples', returned to die and to be resurrected annually, with the going and coming of the sun.

They and all other pre-christian gods slipped into an undertow. They remain to measure our time in *Moon's day, Tew's day, Woden's day, Thor's day, Freya's day, Saturn's day and Sun's day* and in *Janus, Februs, Mars, Avril, Maia, and Juno*. And they are often celebrated coincidentally… for examples, whenever a plastic evergreen is dressed with plastic baubles and plastic tinsel or a Christmas stocking is packed with fruit and nuts.

By the Middle Ages they had become… John Barleycorn – *who is reborn when his blood germinates the Spring-sown seed*, Robin Goodfellow *whose blood is on the robin's breast*; Jack-in-the-Green – The Green Man, *Guardian of Forest and Orchard who leads the May Day Dances*; The Spirits of the Forest and Field; Mab *midwife of dreams*; Pan; Water nymphs, pixies… and later the magical characters in stories by the Brothers Grimm (Buy a lovely rosy-red apple – Think of '*Snow White*' and wash it well!)

Robins, who guarded the apple tree, were fed cyder-soaked cakes as it was wassailed for the next harvest with great noise and bonfires on Twelfth Night. Sometimes cyder-soaked cakes were pushed onto a cow's horns and the cow made to toss them, when forecasts of harvest were made by how and where the cakes landed *'Here's to Thee old apple tree. Whence thou shall bud and whence thou may blow And whence thou may bear apples enow; Hatsful, capsful. Bushel, bushel; sacksful! And my pockets full too! Huzzah. Huzzah!* This 17th century wish shouted three times went country wide; carried in the air – Some of these practices persist **and they work**… but not for the urbane!

The power of 'Apple', as a critical social necessity, waned with the cleaving of town and country by 'Industrial Revolution' but its symbolism remains in our language. For examples… We speak of 'good' and 'bad' apples; what comes of 'one rotten apple in the barrel'; 'Adam's apple'; 'an apple for the teacher', 'the apple of my eye'; 'upsetting the apple-cart', of 'being an 'apple polisher', 'an apple a day'. And the highly toxic *Datura* as 'The Devil's Apple'.

The Franks became Christianised late in the 5th Century and later, when Charles the Magnificent was crowned Holy Roman Emperor in AD800 his empire stretched from the Pyrenees, through northern Italy and to the east of Germany. He encouraged monasteries and Christian learning and Aachen, his capital was as are 'Whitehall' and 'Brussels' today.

Capitulare de Villis set empire-wide standards of high quality, which kept the, otherwise, warring tribes, tied to the land.

Every portion of the empire was required to produce particular quantities of designated foods, which included apples, pears, cherries, plums and peaches and any failure in compliance or failings in quality, brought punishment.

There were thirty or so *permitted* varieties of apple and pear, listed as sweet, sour, scented, early or keeping which were to be grown in orchards of *'regular appearance'*.

He pressurised the 'Heathens' to the north and in doing so, pushed Norse raiders into becoming settlers and much of Britain came to be ruled by a serial ragbag of Angle, Saxon, Jutish, Wightic and Norse Kinglings and ephemeral Federations and High Kings.

Just as a unitary 'England' had come to be, Guillaume 'Le Bátard', Duke of Normandy, led the last successful Viking invasion. These 'Frankified Norsemen' came as conquerors, not settlers and carried out Roman-like asset stripping and imposed Norman-French as the Establishment's language, for hundreds of years… If *'A horse! A horse!'* or *'Once more unto the breach…'* <u>were</u> said, then it was in French… for Henry VIII, was our first monarch to have English as his mother tongue.

The Normans loved high-quality cyder and introduced good Norman varieties – Today, 'Norman' or 'Jersey' in the name of a cyderapple variety suggests good quality. William ruled by State and Church and there was a huge increase in church building. He allowed monastic orders to settle and their *Pomariums* began modern orchard practices, hybridising techniques and apple cuisine.

The notions of gardens, which were designated for 'pleasure' or 'produce', came back with the Crusaders and the rich and powerful of Western Europe copied Moorish practices.

Eleanor of Castille, Edward the First's queen (c.1300) planted her West Country pleasure garden with the fine French late-keeping apple 'Blandurel'.

Charles the First of France (c.1400) planted an orchard with more than a thousand trees including the miniature Paradise Apple. This was much like the Roman 'Golden Gaulish', but it may have been a descendant of a Knights Templar introduction of an Anatolian 'Golden Apple' – Our present day grafting stocks owe much to its genes.

Orchardists began growing for market and at first the English market imported Normandy apples – Court Pendu Gris, Blandurel and Golden Paradise.

Kent developed to become 'The Garden of England' and to supply London's Billingsgate and future markets with both dessert and Costards (hence *costermonger*).

The first **'English'** varieties to be marketed were The Pearmain and The Queening, both being 'improved' cyderapples and apples in variety went out to

Europeans' colonies.

The newly introduced Moorish 'spice', Sugar, popularised the apple as jams and marmalades and its 'heat' was found to be more reliable for fermenting than was honey's.

Sweetmeats 'glittering with icy crystals' became the finish for all good meals.

The Royal Society was founded in 1662 and was of philosopher-scientists, who were engaged in holistic enquiry into Nature. In 1664 a member John Evelyn published his 'Sylva; – or A Discourse of Forest Trees, And the Propagation of Timber in His Majesty's Dominions'. This monumental work was concerned, mostly, with the production of timber for The Navy but included a *Pomona*, which was mainly of apples for cyder and *A Gardener's Almanack*, which detailed by variety and season, apples for the gardener and for market. Brompton Park Nursery, '*Importers and Makers of Apples, Pears, Cherries and Plums*' were his sponsors. Many of their apples were grafted onto the dwarfing 'Paradise', which they supplied to 'gentlefolk' together with 'Espaliers' on more vigorous stocks – These, they recommended, should be alternately of apple and pear to *'delight the prospect for the eye'*.

Landowners came to love wine-quality cyder and part-paid their workers with the 'small-cider', resulting from second and subsequent pressings. The spent pulp supplied seedlings from which to select new varieties and was then recycled through pigs for the land. The labourers had safe water for fieldwork and home, but it was said of small-cider *"If it had been better, we wouldn't have got it and if it had been any worse, we couldn't have stomached it!"* Apples and pears were considered as being similar, so far as cyder was concerned.

In the opinion of the 17th Century connoisseur Beale, *'a mixture of 'crabs and Imny pears' gives a cyder 'finer than all the wines of France'* but *'plain perry purges worse than any Galenist'*.

The 17th Century cyderapple 'Redstreak' – sadly extinct – came from a French cyderapple pip collected and grown by Charles I's Ambassador to France, Lord Scudamore. It is said to have juiced to gravities of around 1080 (11% alcohol), and that it was superior to and preferred to, imported wines – Some wine importers even mixed its cyder with inferior imported wine, to be sold as 'Fine Cyder'.

Richard Harris, gardener to Henry VIII, had introduced palatable pears, but the first 'fine dessert' pear came to Belgium in 1750 and to England in 1820 with Abbé Hardenpont's superb 'Glou Morceau' and *The Pear* became <u>the</u> craze for the French during the 18th Century. French pears remain supreme…

The search for excellence continued and accelerated over the next 200 years. In 1861, **The Royal Horticultural Society** was founded *'to promote the quality and*

17th, 18th & 19th Century Apples at Brogdale

Left to right; top line first:

Bow Hill Pippin	*Diamond Jubilee*	*Granny Gifford*	*Orange Goff*
Beauty of Kent	*Christmas Pearmain*	*Gooseberry*	*Mabott's Pearmain*
Colonel Vaughan	*Castle Major*	*Gascoyne's Scarlett*	*Lamb Abbey*
Faversham Creek	*Benchley Pippin*	*Foster's Seedling*	*Kentish Fillbasket*

range of all produce'. The society promoted excellence in fruit varieties, which continues. Apples became <u>the</u> craze of 19th Century Britain when connoisseurs laid out tables of show apples for tasting after the evening meal, and urged their nurserymen and head gardeners to raise fine new varieties, for admiration and promotion at RHS Shows. Fine and lasting varieties were raised in amateurs' kitchen gardens and The Royal Horticultural Society's dedication to high standards continues, in for examples, the The **RHS Fruit Group**, founded in 1945 and in the ongoing **RHS Trials**.

Apples were judged in terms we would associate now with wine-buffs. For example Morton Shand's father in comparing Cox's with Ribston's... *'A shade too sweet and rather floridly luscious and so lacks the austere aristocratic refinement that Ribston exemplifies transcendentally... beautifully soft but somehow insufficiently rounded and hence not quite perfectly balanced.'*

Very few of us could compare the virtues of these cultivars now, but hopefully more will wish to.

Modern Times and Globalisation

The popularity of the **English Apple**, faltered, under the first onslaught of foreign competition at the beginning of the 20th Century.

Its popularity rallied, led by amongst many others; the nurseryman and connoisseur, E. Bunyard; The RHS Fruit Officer M. Potter; Morton Shand, scholar, linguist, fruit-collector and radio columnist; the composer and fruit collector Gerald Finzi and C. H. Middleton 'The Radio Gardener'. Bunyard promoted our apples according to their qualities of taste and in *The Anatomy of Dessert* (1929) he gave warning, that from ignorance would come a twilight for British apples… *'How often, after a dinner ordered with intelligence, prepared with art and served with distinction and at a table which would scorn an unacknowledged Bordeaux or an invalid Port, do we dwindle to a dessert unworthy of its setting… The American Jonathan!'* He goes on to impress the need *'to wait for Ribston's prime of volatile ethers, of sugars and grateful balance until November'.* And he lists the premium varieties for each season… *'The Summery strawberriness of early Worcester,* to be followed by *'The meltingly fragrant James Grieve';* 'the anise Ellison'; 'that very attar, The Gravenstein';* and in November *'that Chateau Y'quem of an apple, the Cox'* and in December *'the nutty warmth of Blenheim'. 'The aristocratic Rosemary Russet and Claygate Pearmain'* of the New Year and, even in March, a well grown King's Acre Pippin *'could yet show the plump turgescence of youth.'* …Wherever he spoke, he offered varietal tastings from his Allington Fruit Nursery, as did his friend, the gastronome André Simon at his 'Dining Circles' and C. H. Middleton, 'The Radio Gardener', promoted the English Apple on the air.

The campaign had lasting success. When we arrived in Suffolk in 1957, there were still more than a dozen varieties of locally grown apples to be had in succession and half a dozen varieties of pears. There are now, very few to be had here. Suffolk's Conference Centres and Business Parks outnumber its orchards and we count ourselves to be very fortunate in having the space to grow some 30 apple cultivars and ten varieties of pears for our own enjoyment.

Morton Shand and Gerald Finzi collected and saved well over a hundred cultivars, which would have disappeared without their intervention and which are still with us in gardens and collections.

If those connoisseurs were here today assessing the qualities of these foreign fruit-factory things, which fill Store's shelves during our home season, then they would be limited to very pithy descriptions… *'Sweet, juicy, wet, crisp, hard, woolly, cloying, insipid, tinny, empty… 'Le Crunch''* they might say, is followed by *'Le Nothing!'*…

Here and Now

We live in interesting times, when *The Globalised Market* exploits everything and everyone. It manufactures nothing, grows nothing, but controls production, distribution, promotion and livelihoods with super-Olympian amorality.

It runs on inflation, usury, bankruptcy, and creative accounting, asset stripping and a continuing plunder of the Earth's resources. *The Free Global Market* is not fair-trading, but carpet bagging on the grand scale. It pleads Darwinism, but nothing could be less fitted for the survival of Mankind, than to be in complete opposition to omnipotent Nature.

It treats The Earth's resources as infinite and existing only to feed its insatiable appetite. But the Earth and its parts were made finite at The Creation. They have been and may be transmuted in uncountable ways, but everything, animate and inanimate, is of some finite World resources – and temporary.

Nature managed well enough before the coming of Mankind and it will need a deal of science, foresight and moral courage – and not a little altruism – to discourage it from doing so again. W. S. Gilbert's (1836-1911) observation that... Man was Nature's sole mistake... may prove to be very un-comical.

Supermarketing is a tiny thread in globalisation's web and as it was that the Industrial Revolution cut town from country, it was the coming of Supermarkets, which severed the last link between consumer and artisan. It caused not only the demise of local shops, but of 'fruits in season' having any social significance. Supermarkets have brought great diversity to our cuisine, and great convenience, but at what cost?

To put **'The Apple'** into perspective... The Kentucky grower, Frank Browning, reports that the receipts from the sale of **chicken** by the supermarket Wal-Mart (Owner of ASDA) in <u>one</u> United State of America, exceeds the value of the entire American Apple industry. Generations of his family have grown apples, but now he and all other 'local' growers in the USA, are in peril from... 'The crass and tacky laws of the marketplace, which promote and prefer the supermarket's bland and forced, assembly line 'commodities', to Real Apples, grown to perfection and marketed in a neighbourhood.'... ('Apples' 2000)

Successive governments of ours repeat the mantra – '<u>Only</u> if it is in Britain's Interests'. Now, how can it in be the **Earth's** interests, let alone Britain's, to encourage the destruction of any nation's resources and to compound the damage, by squandering fossil fuel and exacerbating the fouling of an already fouled environment? Clearly it makes short term market profit, but it defies common sense to import that which you can grow or manufacture at home... What happens when the oil stops flowing? As Roger Bacon's Brazen Head spoke long ago, before it dashed itself 'Time was. Time is. Time is past!'

In the spring of 2002, the organic gardeners' *Henry Doubleday Research Association* reported a 20-nation promotion of 'Food Sovereignty' – a concept which includes the rights of peoples to decide their own agricultural and food policies, to arrange their own manners of trading and to impose their own standards for food safety. It is to be hoped that it will prevail over *The General Agreement on Tariffs and Trade (GATT)* and other of globalisation's 'agreements', which appropriate these rights.

There are other bright signs for change... Sainsbury's fund Open Days at Brogdale, Waitrose have 'adopted' an apple cultivar and many supermarket chains give lip service to supporting British Fruit. These are tiny victories for home producers, but nowhere nearly sufficient to drive a revival. Now is the time to press for rather more from major retailers... They are our principal providers – and we are theirs... Market forces? They are said to be us.

The last refuges for most apples and pears of distinction are in collections and kitchen gardens and with the few persistent and dedicated orchardists who grow for local markets. I fear that the English orchard industry approaches that critical mass from which it cannot recover. – But maybe not and if it rallies again there will be stocks of connoisseur-cultivars waiting in kitchen gardens and collections for our descendants to savour in season.

The first step towards solving a problem is to realise that there is one.

'...*Look around people, wherever you roam – and admit that the waters around you have grown*'
(Bob Dylan, Folk Singer)

★ Flowering plants began between 120 and 80 million years ago.

★ Apples, pears, quinces, medlars and other pomes belong to 'The Rose' Superorder.

★ Modern apple varieties began in Turkmenistan, Uzbekistan and Khirgizia.

★ Domestic pears and apples do not share, completely, the same gene-sets as perrypears and cyderapples.

★ Present-day civilisations stem from Sumer and Harappa and share recognition of Nature's powers.

★ The Romans developed grafting and the Normans laid the bases for modern orchard practices.

★ The Royal Society was founded in 1662 and began a holistic investigation of Nature and Man's condition.

★ The Royal Horticultural Society was formed in 1861, dedicated to the search for excellence.

★ The Industrial Revolution and supermarkets have separated consumer from artisan.

★ Nature is omnipotent.

CHAPTER TWO

A Selection of Cultivars

Bramley blossom

The modern English apple may be seen to begin with the introduction of Cox's Orange Pippin in 1825. This coincided, by happenstance with the passing of mediaeval practices, when 'The Last Witch in England', Isaac Stebbins, was 'swum for a witch' in The Grimmer on Wickham Skeith Green in Suffolk.

My maternal great-great-grandfather, William Farmer, was living at that time and had already deserted his village for a 'better' life in industrial Birmingham.

Cox's Orange Pippin was raised from the Ribston Pippin of 1707, which is thought to have been a seedling from a 'reinette' pip, brought back from Rouen by Sir Henry Goodricke of Ribston Hall. The original Ribston blew down in 1928.

Intermediate with Ribston and Cox's are the chance seedlings Blenheim Orange (1740 Oxon.) and Bramley's Seedling (c.1810 Notts.) and these four cultivars remain to be the measure for all others. I recall that my grandfather considered Ribston to be peerless as an eating apple and he thought Blenheim to be the best for eating with cheese and the equal of Bramley's for cooking.

It is significant that the majority of really worthwhile cultivars are <u>old or very old</u> and were raised during a time when raisers were seeking excellence. Most of well-funded modern breeding research has been and is concerned with, primarily, appearance and crop potential.

'Taste' it is opined, is 'subjective' and cannot be bred for. **But of course 'taste' is subjective!** – But the comparison must be between cultivars of similar stature…

For example Cox's, Ashmead's Kernel, Ribston's, Orleans Reinette and Sunset have comparably complex but differing flavours, which may be ranked according to individual appeal. Just as Empire may be compared with Jonathan, since they are both of a similarly simple nature and typical of 'The Market's' desire for blandness – cultivars, which are attractive to the eye and neither offend nor delight the palate… Fruit's parallel with *'Fat free, salt free… taste free'* …*(With added chilli or sugar)*. Surely it is the choice of parents, which is 'subjective' for, whereas 'Cox'. 'Ribston' and their like, pass on measures of complex flavours to their seedlings, 'Empires' and 'Jonathans', pass on their capability for huge crops of factory-orchard plonk.

Why do you not see American Cox', Ribston, Blenheim or Rosemary Russet on the shelves? Simply because they will come to perfection only in our gentle maritime climate and will not suffer forced factory treatment. Why do you see only token British as Cox and Egremont? Because they are very well known and prized for their qualities and were adopted by supermarkets when they began.

Most of us have an expectancy of qualities by sight. Presentation experts would have it that 'shiny, bright, red or green and supersize, have immediate 'apple-customer' appeal and supermarkets' displays suggest that they may be correct. If attractive yet vapid cultivars persist at the expense of better, then fewer and fewer customers will realise that better exist.

I am with Jane Grigson, who said that for her, apples, which were offered as dessert, and *'bright red and shiny'*, meant that a plastic skin was covering *'a woolly and collapsing flesh'* and *'bright green and shiny'* suggested, *'hard, with an underdeveloped flavour'* which *'may improve with cooking'*. *'Russets'* she said, *'or red or orange flushed apples with russetting are generally the most rewarding'*. For examples… *Cox, Blenheim Orange, Orlean's Reinette, Charles Ross, Belle de Boskoop, Calville Blanc, Ellison's Orange and Devonshire Quarrenden'*… *'All these and what do we get?'* said she – *'Golden Delicious – not the most pleasing experience!'* But believed that *'Whatever you buy from the supermarket, should improve with a little storage – so buy, ahead'*.

In my opinion, the best way to repair our loss, is to encourage the growing of good cultivars, by rejecting all foreign apples which are imported <u>during our own season</u> and demanding the stocking of only <u>'real' English apples in the English Apple Season</u>… (September-March). Any preferential treatment given to imports over similar, let alone far superior home-grown produce, undermines the livelihoods of our own growers and eventually, of all of us. If such were encouraged in other than business it would be called treason. Other exporting countries do not encourage such practice at home… for example: The Republic of Ireland Government encourages its population to buy local produce whenever there is a choice.

Change may take some time. Better grow your own!

There are over 5,000 named varieties of apples and so all lists are bound to be selective and my selection comes from three sources:

1. Varieties recommended by Rosanne Sanders in 'The English Apple' – some of which, by established reputation, have the highest or particular qualities and others, which are considered to be of promise and are indicated thus*

2. Are in my own collection, but not listed in (1).
   And...

3. Newer cultivars.

Wherever possible, the source for the descriptions is Joan Morgan and Allison Richards 'The Book of Apples' but includes, mostly gardening, rather than other purely botanical information.

Key to the Selection

Dessert and Culinary Apple

Appearance and Use

Each cultivar is followed by its appearance (1-8). This classification, which is based on appearance and purpose, comes from Bultitude's development of Bunyard's classification.

1. Green, smooth skinned, acidic, culinary... example Lord Derby

2. Predominantly green, may have orange flush, smooth, sweet, dessert... Sturmer

3. Flushed &/or striped, smooth, acidic, culinary... Bramley's Seedling

4. Flushed &/or striped, smooth, primarily dessert, maybe dual purpose... Gravenstein

5. Predominantly yellow, sweet &/or acid, dessert/culinary... Golden Delicious

6. Predominantly red flushed, smooth, sweet, dessert... Worcester Pearmain

7. Flushed and striped, some russet, usually sweet, dessert... Cox's Orange Pippin

8. Almost or completely russet, usually sweet, dessert... Egremont Russet

Classification

Each cultivar's class (1-8) is followed by its season... Early, Mid or Late and Dessert, Culinary or **CD** or **DC** and its Pollination Group 1, 2, 3 or 4.

All apples will juice, but those, which have been recommended by The Long Ashton Research Station, are noted as J and (A)cid, (M)id-acid or (S)weet.

Most varieties may be pollinated by <u>any variety but themselves</u>, which is within the group or in the groups either side, but <u>Triploid varieties do not produce useful pollen</u> and have the need for two other compatible varieties. Tetraploids have no need for special requirement.

A few cultivars are self-pollinating and may be planted alone. They are labelled **SP**.

Biennial and irregular bearers are not reliable pollinators. If there is limited space then plant a 'Family tree'. For examples… **Adam's Pearmain** 7 LD 3 *, may be pollinated by and will pollinate, any cultivar in Groups 2, 3 or 4, but…

Bramley's Seedling 3 LC 3 Triploid JA *, will accept pollen from any variety in Groups 2, 3, or 4 but is unable to give useful pollen.

Fruit sizes refer to Large (7.5-8cm) Medium (5-7cm) and Small (below 5cm) and the tree growth is described as weak, medium, vigorous and upright or spreading. 'Season' refers to the maximum period, which can be expected from storage in a cool apple shed, but will vary with seasonal conditions.

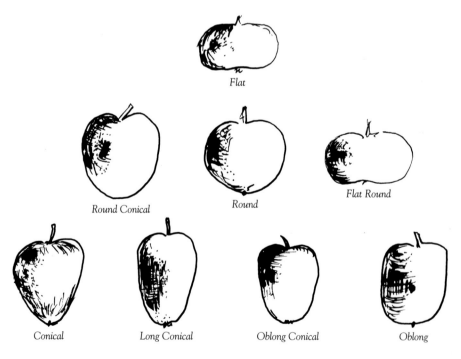

Flat

Round Conical

Round

Flat Round

Conical

Long Conical

Oblong Conical

Oblong

APPLE SHAPES

Bramley in bloom

The Cultivars

Adam's Pearmain 7 LD 3 *

Hereford, 1826. Handsome, rich, nutty, firmly textured, conical fruit of medium size. Greatly prized by Victorian connoisseurs. Excellent garden tree with particularly attractive flowers. Fruit has an orange flush over yellow/gold stripes, with some russet and speckles. Good crops. Pick e/mOct. Season Nov-Mar.

Allington Pippin 7 L DC 3 Biennial

Laxton's, 1884. King of the Pippins X Cox's Orange Pippin Fruitdrop-pineapple flavour, still sharp at Christmas and needs to have had a good year to ripen. Said to remain sharp in the Midlands Very sharp in Nov, but cooks well retaining shape, with a very good flavour. We liked it, but, alas, our tree blew down! Fruit brownish-red over pale yellow becoming orange over bright yellow, some russet. Does not store well. Size medium with cream flesh. Tree of average vigour, crops well. Pick eOct. Season Nov-Dec.

Annie Elizabeth 3 LC 4 *

S. Greatorex, Clerk, Leicester 1857. Round to round-oblong fruit of medium size. Named after his deceased daughter. Claimed as Blenheim Orange Seedling.

Original tree died 1970. A common market apple until the 1930s and remains popular in the North. Highly regarded long keeping culinary apple. Keeps shape when cooked and needs little if any added sugar. Excellent show apple with very pretty maroon/purple flowers. Greasy skin with orange red flush and many short red stripes over greenish yellow gold. Flesh white, sharp.

A hardy tree but drops fruit easily in wind. Excellent late cooker. We have found our tree to be an unreliable cropper but not biennial. We enjoy it when we have it! Pick e/mOct. Use Nov-Apr.

Annie Elizabeth

Arthur Turner 5 EC 3

Charles Turner, Nurseryman, 1912. Cooks to a pale yellow well-flavoured puree without much need for sugar. Splendid early pie and sauce apple and bakes well. Fine garden variety. Large mid-conical fruit with a brownish flush over pale yellow with pale cream flesh. Average vigour. Pick Sept. Season Sept-Nov.

Ashmead's Kernel 8 LD 4 *

Dr Ashmead, Glos. c.1700. Strong sweet-sharp, with intense acid/fruit-drop flavours. A long esteemed connoisseur's apple, often scoring over Cox. A med-flat-round apple of completely dull russet. In my opinion a reliable and splendid apple of dull appearance. Of average vigour to pick e/mOct. Season Dec-Feb.

Ashmead's Kernel

Ballerina

East Malling, 1976. Trade name for markedly columnar Wijcik Mackintosh crosses 'Bolero' 'Polka' 'Maypole' and 'Waltz'. Useful as decorative patio trees, but without any commendable fruit qualities when grown in UK.

Blackmoor Russet see **Norfolk Royal**

Blenheim Orange 7 L CD 3 Triploid Biennial *

A chance seedling discovered by Kempster against Blenheim Palace wall and named Kempster's Pippin in 1740, but the Duke of Marlborough, graciously allowed its name to be changed when its worth became apparent. Nutty, sweet, crumbly. Excellent with cheese. Large fruit cooks to a stiff puree and makes good 'Charlotte' Becomes a powerful looking tree whose hard wood was used for cog-railway wheels. The flat-round slightly ribbed fruit has an orange red flush with a few stripes over greenish yellow-gold. Cropping tends towards being biennial and the variety has some resistance to mildew. Pick lSept-Oct. Season Oct-Jan.

Bountiful 4 MC 3 *

East Malling Res. Inst. 1964. Cox's Orange Pippin X Lane's Prince Albert. Light, juicy, soft sweet. Just about keeps shape when cooked. Tree of average vigour with resistance to mildew giving a heavy crop in lSept. Season Sept-Nov.

Braeburn 4 LD 4

G. Moore, New Zealand, 1952. Chance seedling. Refreshing crisp, firm NZ commercial apple. Has tended to fail in UK but a clone (Blackmoor is a stockist) is said to ripen good crops in normal UK seasons. Of average vigour and spreading habit. Pick lOct. Season Jan-Mar.

Bramley

Bramley's Seedling
3 LC 3 Triploid * JA

Mary Anne Brailsford, Notts, c.1810. Cooks to a strongly flavoured and acid pale cream puree which will not be shaded by the most sugary or spicy recipe. In storage the acidity attenuates to sufficiently sweet for some to like as dessert. It is not to everyone's taste but I find it to be without peer as a culinary apple. Modern commercial examples seem poorer in every respect but appearance. It is becoming increasingly susceptible to scab and bitterpit and at some time in the future it may be preferable to grow an alternative… for example, Dumelow's Seedling. Striking bright pink flowers. Fruit large flat-round greenish yellow with brownish flush, broad red stripes and some russet dots – commercial fruit is often without russet. Pick e/mOct. Season Nov-lFeb. commercially -Jun. Crimson Bramley Notts., sport 1913Is catalogued by some and differs only in colour.

Catshead   1   LC   3

Parkinson, England, 1629. Quite like a cat's head in profile. Cooks to a firm sharp puree. Box shaped fruit made it useful for farmworkers' dumplings. The green to pale yellow fruit is large to very large with some russet dots. The tree is of average vigour and spreading. Pick eOct. Season Oct-Jan.

Charles Ross   4   CD   3   JM   SP

C. Ross, Berks, c.1890. Peasegood Nonesuch X Cox's Orange Pippin, which does well as far north as Scotland. Light aromatic juicy firm flesh. Keeps shape when cooked and has a sweet, pear-like flavour. Best used early for cooking. Handsome, medium to large conical fruit. Orange-red flush with broken red stripes over greenish-yellow. Some russet patches. Recommended by Jane Grigson. Pick mSept. Season lSept-December.

Cornish Aromatic   7   LD   4

Noticed by Sir Christopher Hawkins, Cornwall 1817, but probably much older. Needs a good season to reach its potential. Very handsome and at its best a firm fleshed, sweet-sharp, pear flavoured and spicy, but it can be good-looking, flavourless and chewy. The fruit is medium-large, with a bright red flush and faint red stripes over gold, with much russet netting. It makes a medium tree with light crops. My experience of quality is much the same, but when it is good it is really, really good! – But it has always had reasonable crops. Pick mOct. Season Dec-Feb.

Cornish Aromatic

Cornish Gilliflower 7 LD 4 *

Truro, c.1800. Chance seedling. Knobbly with yellow perfumed flesh. In late October it is intensely flavoured, rich and aromatic, becoming later, delicate and flowery. Very highly prized by the Victorians and remains a good garden tree. Fruit is medium sized ribbed oblong-conical and has a dark red flush over gold and fine russet dots and patches. Pick mOct. Season Nov-Feb.

Court Pendu Plat 7 LD 4

France. Described by Baulin 1613 but older. Rich, fruity pineapple acidity, which becomes sweetly scented but still powerfully flavoured by February. It has remained a favourite for centuries both in France and here and no blame can be given to the French for preferring to export the 'Le Crunch' – the wet, bland Golden Delicious – and keeping this superlative apple for themselves! The medium to small fruit has pale cream flesh and is flushed with stripy red markings over a greenish yellow to bright yellow ground. The upright tree is of average vigour and crops well. Pick mOct. Season Dec/Jan-Apr.

Cox's Orange Pippin 7 LD 3 *

R. Cox, Retired Brewer, 1825. Believed to be a Ribston seedling. Perfectly ripe it is deliciously sweet-acid, aromatic, spicy, honeyed, nutty and pear-like and it is of the most beautifully subtle complexity of flavour. As early as 1982 Jane Grigson complained of how it was being downgraded by overcropping and by the growing of 'improved' strains. ('New' or 'Improved' – are usually anodyne for 'Poorer, but cheaper to produce'.) This undermining of the variety has been further exacerbated by bureaucrats' insistence that size determines quality grade. The ideal Cox is a <u>small medium to medium</u>-sized apple and its flavour and texture are changed for the worse by forcing it to grow larger. But, even in its diluted form, it remains without peer amongst the foreign, celluloid skinned and bland varieties with which it is compelled to compete during its British season. Its fruit should have an orange flush with red stripes over greenish yellow, turning gold with russet dots and patches. Older cultivars have russet in the stem basin and in the eye. Howard Stringer (Brogdale) considers that removing russet to 'improve' the appearance has removed 'russet's' nuance from the flavour. Some local markets still have access to unimproved Cox, but I fear it will be lost. I had, once, a surfeit of Cox' and I made it into the most disappointing single varietal cyder that I have ever tasted!… Horses for courses!

It is exceptionally prone to most apple ills and cannot be grown without repeated spraying throughout the season. It is not to be recommended to other than masochist gardeners, (**Sunset** approaches its quality and is much more easily grown) – but do lobby main retailers for less polished and oversized specimens. Do buy your tree from older clones grown by specialist fruit stock growers. Pick lSept-Oct. Season mOct-Jan. Commerce April. **Cherry Cox, Crimson Cox, King Cox, Queen Cox** and various **Clonal Cox** are offered as improvements but are not necessarily so.

D'Arcy Spice   8   LD   4   *

Tolleshunt D'Arcy, Essex, c.1785. Hot, spicy and nutmeg-like by the New Year, but only after a good sunny season. The firm white flesh becomes spongy but the flavour remains. Tradition has it picked on Guy Fawkes Day and stored in sacks hung on the tree (ours go into the apple store) Still favoured in Essex and grown for local marketing. The greenish-white fleshed, rather dry fruit is medium sized, oblong ribbed and bright to dull yellowish-green with large ochre russet patches sometimes with purplish hue, and of a generally unappealing appearance. The skin can become leathery. The tree is of average vigour and the cropping is said to be erratic. I have not found this to be the case for our tree always crops well and annually. Pick lOct (I pick e/mNov). Season Jan-Mar.

Destivale

An early mid season bright red flushed apple, offered by Marshalls and said to have an exceptionally fine flavour. Pick and eat in September. No other details.

Devonshire Quarrenden   6   ED   2   Somewhat Biennial

Introduce to Devon from France (Carentan), 1676. Distinctly sweet winey strawberry/loganberry taste with good acidity. Must be 'caught', for it softens quickly. Hardy in Scotland. The fruit is flat-round, medium to small dark crimson over a yellow background. I like it straight from the tree – when you must catch it sometime! Useful for early juice to blend in early cyder. Pick and use Aug.

Discovery   6   ED   3   *

Mr. Dummer, Fruit Worker, Essex, 1949. Worcester Pearmain X *poss* Beauty of Bath. Needs to be well ripened on the tree to show its fair and faintly strawberry flavour. The flesh is crisp and juicy and often pink flushed. It has bright red flushed skin over a greenish to yellow background. It was a popular early variety for local sale in the 1980s. It is better than its parents. It is partially tip bearing and slow to fruit. Pick and eat mAug-eSept.

Dumelow's Seedling   3   LC   4

Raised by Richard Dumeller, Ashby, Leicestershire, late 1700's. (Probably

Northern Greening X) as 'Dumelow's Crab' Fruit pale greenish-white, sometimes with apricot dots and purplish lenticles and a few stripes. It becomes greasy in store. Cooks like Bramley but creamier. An excellent baking apple and considered to be the best for mincemeat. A premier Victorian culinary apple but overtaken in commerce by Bramley, which is less acid.It is a good garden apple and it may become easier to source, as Bramley becomes increasingly susceptible to bitter pit and scab. It retains its brisk acidity through the spring. Hardy in the North where it is called 'The May Day Apple'. Synonyms Wellington; Normanton Wonder. Harvest m/lOct. Season Nov-April.

Egremont Russet 8 MD 2 *

Scott's Nurserymen, Merriot, Somerset, 1872. Very distinctively 'russet' for its cream flesh is smoky, nutty flavoured, lightly tannic and juicy, becoming dry. Morton Shand – fruit and wine collector, connoisseur and broadcaster – recalled it as being like the scent of crushed fern. It was popularised by Bunyard as *'one of the richest and most prettily coloured late autumn fruits.'* It is available in supermarkets, fortunately, where customers have been trained to recognise 'Total russet' or 'Total

Egremont Russet

absence of russet' as 'Good', but smoother 'polished' and less russety fruit is becoming common. The fruit is medium size and flat-round and totally ochre russet over gold and with a hint of orange flush. Of upright habit it is very hardy and resistant to scab but susceptible to bitter pit. It crops well and makes very pleasant juice. Pick lSept-Oct. Season Oct-Dec.

Ellison's Orange 7 MD 4 SP

Rev. Ellison, Lincs, 1904. Cox's Orange Pippin X Calville Blanc. The tree is average in vigour and has a very showy flourish. At its best it is reckoned to be the most glorious of apples by those who appreciate its aniseed overtone. It has an intensely aromatic flavour and develops into a melting juicy cream flesh. It does not store well and can be reminiscent of cough mixture. The fruit is of medium size and ribbed mid conical. It has red stripes over a yellow-green-gold greasy base. A good cropper and hardy. Pick m/lSept. Season lSept-lOct.

Encore 1/3 LC 3 *

Charles Ross, Berks, 1906. Believed to be Warner's King X Northern Greening. Large fruit. Used early is very acid, later makes creamy richly flavoured baked apple without need for much sugar. Good garden variety. Beautiful large deep pink flowers. Of average vigour it crops well and is resistant to scab. Pick e/mOct. Season Dec-Apr.

Falstaff 4 LD 3 JM

Dr Alston EMRS, Kent, 1965. James Grieve X Golden Delicious. Pretty with a red flush and stripes. Fruity well balanced, crisp and juicy. Average sized tree. Frost resistant and a heavy cropper. Pick eOct. Season Oct-Dec. **Red Falstaff** has similar qualities.

Fiesta 7 MD 3 *

Dr Alston EMRS, Kent, 1972. Cox Orange Pippin X Ida Red. Quite Cox-like. But much easier to grow and is frost resistant. It is well-balanced rich, sweet, acid, aromatic, crisp, and juicy but has a tough skin. It becomes empty and tasteless with keeping. It crops heavily and it has far more disease resistance than Cox. Pick lSept. Season Oct-Jan. Comm. -May.

Gala 6 LD 4 *

J. Hutton-Kidd, NZ, 1954. Kidd's Orange Red X Golden Delicious. The cream flesh is rich, honeyed, juicy and with some of the perfume of Kidd's. The more colourful **Royal Gala** (after Queen Elizabeth) is grown here. The medium sized fruit is oblong-conical bright red flushed with redder stripes over gold with fine russet spots. The blossom is most attractive and the average sized tree bears well but is prone to canker. **Mondial** and other clones are said to suit our climate. Pick eOct. Season Oct-Jan/Mar.

George Cave 4 ED 2 *

G. Cave, Essex, 1923. A strong sweet-sharp taste makes more interesting as a summer apple than the Beauty of Bath which it used to follow when we had apples in their season. The medium to small round-conical fruit has a red flush and carmine stripes over a greenish-yellow base and a few russet dots and can be prone to cracking. The cropping is good. Pick and eat e/mAug.

George Neal 3 E CD 2 *

Mrs. Reeves, Kent, 1904. Named for G. Neal, Nurseryman. Refreshingly brisk eating apple, pale cream cooked slices keep their shape and have a sweet delicate flavour requiring no sugar. Popular Garden variety. The large flat-round fruit is green turning to pale-yellow with a brownish-red flush. It has beautiful bright pink flowers and the tree is of average vigour Cropping is good and picking is e/mAug. Season Aug-Sept.

Golden Delicious   5   LD   3

H. Mullins, West Virginia, c.1890. *Poss*. Grimes Golden seedling. At best, honeyed, with crisp, juicy, perfumed and almost yellow flesh, but not when grown in UK, for it needs a warmer climate, nor when for export to the UK, it is picked whilst immature. Although a warm clime apple it develops a remarkably tough skin and has little flavour when grown 'hot' and picked early.

If it is left on the tree in such provenances as Kentucky or Virginia until it is golden and has had time to build up sugars, it is a <u>fair</u> apple. That the UK market is a dump for its huge crops, is in great measure, because it travels well, has a long shelf life and because it is an excellent pollinator. Much used for baby foods and commercial pies, for bland apple juice and as a bulker in some so-called ciders. It makes a spreading tree with very pretty flowers but it is not worth garden space. I am in total agreement with Geoffrey Smith, onetime BBC Gardener, who said that *'It be at its best, composted and laid around a Cox!'*. Pick lOct. Season Nov-Jan.

Golden Noble   5   MC   3   *

P. Flannigan, a Head Gardener, Norfolk, 1820 but possibly W. Perfect, Nursery-man, Yorks, 1769. Not as acid as Bramley. Cooks to a sharpish, well flavoured puree, bakes well and needs little sugar. Good creamy texture in pies. By spring is a brisk, rich almost dessert apple. Highly prized as a cooker by Victorians and Edwardians. The large round to round/conical fruit is pale light-green turning gold with a little russet. It is a partial tip bearer and it has beautiful flowers. Pick eOct. Season until Mar.

Gravenstein   4   M   DC   1   Triploid

Claimed as from garden of Duke Augustenberg of Schleswig-Holstein c.1600. Savoury crisp but juicy, melting flesh. Keeps shape when cooked, but early picked fruit cooks to a delicious frothy puree. Too large to be classed 'dessert' and

Crimson Gravenstein

not sharp enough to be a 'good' cooker is nevertheless highly prized in North Europe and Canada (which used to export it to UK) We like our **Red Gravenstein** for its strikingly large white flowers and for early fluffy stewed apple, pies and juice and, when just right, eaten from the tree. It makes a vigorous hardy tree. Pick eSept. Season Sept-eOct.

Greensleeves 5 MD 3 * JM SP

Dr F. Alston EMRS, Kent, 1966. James Grieve X Golden Delicious. Has the sweetness of Golden Delicious balanced by the sharpness of James Grieve. Early in the season it is hard and sharp but becomes sweeter and softer. Found in farm-shops and is a popular garden variety. Its fruit is medium sized and pale greenish yellow/yellow and is oblong or mid-conical and slightly ribbed. The flowers are handsome and it crops heavily and early. Pick mSept. Season from the tree and until Oct.

Grenadier   1 EC 3

Origin unknown. Recorded Charles Turner, Nurseryman, 1862. Promoted as an improvement on Keswick Codlin but lacks its sweetness. Cooks to a sharp puree. It is offered now as 'the earliest' culinary apple. The large mid-conical and ribbed fruit is greenish yellow. It crops heavily in mid August. Season Aug-Sept.

Holstein 7 LD 3 Triploid *

Herr Validik, Teacher, Holstein, c.1918. Intensely rich aromatic flavour similar to a good Ribston but like a Cox in appearance. Stronger flavour than Cox but sharper and more coarsely textured. The fruit has an orange red flush with broad red stripes over gold with russet dots. It is medium large and round-conical. A spreading tree which crops well but is prone to frost damage, mildew and canker. Pick lSept-Oct. Season lOct-Jan.

Howgate Wonder 3 LC 4 JA

C. Wratten, Gardener, IOW, c.1915. Makes a large spreading tree resistant to mildew. Quite pleasantly sweet and crisp when eaten fresh and cooks to keep its shape, but it is insipid in comparison with Bramley. Makes a good exhibition apple. The fruit is large to very large, short to mid-conical and five-crowned. It is brownish red with red stripes over green turning to bright orange over yellow and becoming greasy. Pick e/mOct. Season Nov-Mar.

Irish Peach 4 ED 2 *

Sent to London Horticultural Society from Sligo by John Robertson in 1819.

Irish Peach

James Grieve

Ideally eaten from the tree when, if perfect, it is said to have a rich balance of acidity and sweetness with peach overtones. Popular with Victorians for its prettiness in the dessert display. The fruit has a brownish red flush and flecks over a pale yellow ground. The fruit is medium sized. It is the tip bearer of tip bearers and I have been told that the best pruning regime is to cut out the whole branch, which has borne, to a basal bud. I have had little success with my tree and I believe it may be that East Anglia is too far from wet Sligo! This is supported by last year, a wet one for Suffolk, having been its best. Pick and eat in Aug.

James Grieve   4 E DC   3   * JM   SP

J. Grieve, Manager, Dickson's Nursery, Edinburgh, 1893. *Possibly* seedling of Pott's Seedling or Cox. Savoury, deliciously scented, juicy, yet melting flesh, which can be very sharp early in the season. The acidity mellows and the flesh softens but the fine flavour remains. It was a much enjoyed market apple but bruises too easily for modern store handling and it was a pollinator for Cox. The fruit is red flushed and striped over pale green-yellow and is medium sized mid-conical and slightly ribbed with pale cream flesh. It makes a hardy, spreading tree, which is prone to canker. Our two trees have been martyrs to canker for many years but always crop and we look forward to this apple. It makes a rich juice. Pick e/mSept. Season Sept-Oct but may keep until Dec.

Jonagold, Jonagored, New Jonagold and Red Jonagold   4   LD   4   Triploid   *

New York State, Apple Experimental Station, 1941. Golden Delicious X Jonathan. Attractive, more acid than Jonathan and better flavoured than Golden Delicious and almost aromatic, but all too often, metallic and flat. They are widely grown commercially all over the world for their very heavy crops. A medium to large apple with many highly coloured sports. It makes a medium tree prone to canker. Neither of its parents are suitable for UK culture and in my opinion, no progeny from this pairing to date is worthy of a British garden. Pick m-Oct. Season Nov-Jan.

Jubile

A crispy, rosy apple, which is said by Marshalls to have an 'aromatic aftertaste'. Pick October. Season Oct-Dec. No other details.

Jupiter   7   MD   3   Triploid   *

Dr F. Alston EMRS, Kent, 1966. Cox's Orange Pippin X Starking Delicious. Intensely flavoured, aromatic but more robust taste than Cox. Sweet, juicy, loosely textured flesh. A heavy cropper with a tendency to biennial bearing and misshapen fruit. An average sized tree. Pick Oct. Season lOct-Jan.

Katy (Katja) 6 ED 3 J

Balsglad Fruit Breeding Station, Sweden, 1947. James Grieve X Worcester Pearmain. Has some of Worcester's strawberry flavour and firmness but with plenty of Grieve's acidity, but like Worcester it soon goes soft. A farmshop apple and a good juicer. The medium sized, mid-conical fruit is flushed bright red, with red stripes over greenish yellow, becoming yellow, base. An average grower of good crops. Pick eSept. Season Sept-eOct.

Kent (Malling Kent) 6 ED 3

H. M. Tydeman EMRS, Kent, 1949. Cox's Orange Pippin X Jonathan. At best, aromatic, with lots of sugar and acidity to become sweeter and scented by the New Year, but often with a very tough skin and coarse flesh. It betrays its Jonathan blood after a poor year when it has a poor metallic flavour. The medium, round to round-conical fruit is flushed dark orange-red with red stripes over yellow and has a pale cream flesh. It has a very pretty flourish and is of average vigour. The crops are heavy but are prone to coarse russetting. Pick m/lOct. Season Nov-Feb. Commerce June.

Keswick Codlin 5 EC 2 Biennial SP

Gleaston Castle, Lancs rubbish heap, 1793. Cooks to a creamy froth and needs little sugar. Considered by Victorians as <u>the</u> jelly apple and a fine cooker, a refreshing eater and good for juicing. It flowers profusely and makes a neat tree, which was recommended, for arbours and tunnels. It is one of the many, mostly local and unnamed, 'codlins' once prized for early frothy 'coddled' (stewed) apple. There was an ancient, cankered tree when we came in 1957 but it blew down and is yet to be replaced. It is well worth having a codlin, <u>if you can find one</u>. The fruit is conical to oblong-conical and of medium size. It has a pale green-yellow flush over darker yellow and gives regular heavy crops in mAug. Season lAug-Oct.

Kidd's Orange Red 7 LD 3

J. Hutton-Kidd, NZ, 1924. Cox's Orange Pippin X Delicious. Kidd was a retired farmer and fruit breeder who attempted to breed American colour into English taste. A strongly aromatic, rich sweet-acid apple, which mellows to have an intensely flowery rose petal – some say Parma violets – quality. It needs plenty of autumn sun to build up sugars and flavour and is only recommended for the south. We have had very good results in Suffolk in some years. The medium sized,

Kidd's Orange Red

slightly ribbed, five crowned fruit has a deep pinky-crimson flush and darker stripes over a pale-yellow to gold ground with some russet dots. The tree is of average vigour and has a beautiful flourish. The crop potential is good but the tree is prone to canker. **Captain Kidd** is more highly coloured.

Lady Henniker 7 L CD 4

Lord Henniker's Estate, Suffolk, from cyder pommace, c.1845. Brisk, crumbling, deep cream-greenish flesh. Cooks to pale lemon strongly flavoured puree, hardly needing sugar. Victorians used it in their mixed fruit decorations, when *'Its appearance by lamplight, was most striking'* and it was, *'recommended for the artistic orchard'*. It makes a large tree and crops well. Pick eOct. Season Nov-Jan.

Lane's Prince Albert 3 LC 3

Thomas Squire, Herts. Before 1841. Said to be Russet Nonpariel X Dumelow's Seedling. It makes a spreading tree of average stature, which is prone to mildew but resistant to scab. It cooks to a lemon puree, but is not as strongly flavoured as Bramley. Becomes sweeter and even milder, but if overcooked it can become tough. It was originally 'Victoria and Albert' commemorating the Royals' visit to change horses at Squire's Inn, but

Lane's Prince Albert

Thos. Lane, Nurseryman, who distributed it, altered the name for self-advertisement. The fruit bruises easily, but it is undemanding and reliable for the amateur. We find that, although inferior to Bramley, its longer storage potential stretches our stewed apple season! Its fruit is shiny green with some orange-red flush and is mid-conical and of medium size. Pick mOct. Season Nov-eMar.

Laxton's Epicure 7 ED 3

Laxton's Bros, Nurserymen, Beds, 1909. Wealthy X Cox's Orange Pippin. Delicately sweet, juicy and aromatic. Combines some of Cox with the better colour of Wealthy. Good garden and farmshop apple. The fruit is medium to small and mid-conic, with a dark orange-red flush and thick red stripes over greenish yellow. Tree of average size giving heavy crops which is prone to bitter pit. Pick lAug. Season Aug-lSept. **Epicurean** is more highly coloured.

Laxton's Fortune 7 ED 3 Biennial * JM

Laxton's Bros, Nurserymen, Beds, 1904. Cox's Orange Pippin X Wealthy. At best when it has been left on the tree to fully colour and mature. Light, sweet, aromatic and juicy. If picked too soon it is wooden and empty. At one time a Cox pollinator but now confined to gardens and farmshops. It is a medium sized short round-conical apple and is flushed red with short red stripes over greenish yellow to pale yellow with some russet. It makes a hardy tree of average vigour giving good crops. Fruit bruises easily. Pick eSept. Season Sept-Oct. **Fisher Fortune** and **Red Fortune** are more highly coloured.

Laxton's Superb 7 LD 4 Biennial

Laxton Bros, Nurserymen, Beds, 1897. Wyke's Pippin X Cox's Orange Pippin. Has some of the rich complexity of Cox, but with more sweetness with finely textured juicy flesh. It was once a market apple but its biennial nature was its downfall. Nevertheless it is much easier to grow than Cox and makes a rewarding garden apple. The medium sized mid-conical fruit has a deep reddish-purple flush with red stripes over greenish-yellow and with russet dots. The spreading tree is of average size and tends to have whippy new growth and gives heavy, if irregular crops. Pick e/mOct. Season Nov-Jan.

Lord Derby 1 MC 4 SP

R. W. William, Nurseryman, Ches, 1862. Said to be a Catshead seedling. Cooked early, very sharp, needing sugar and makes good pies. Becomes mellower but best cooked green. Very useful in North where it remains green until December. Still a market apple in the North and Scotland. Large and oblong-conical it is green with a pinkish tinge. Makes a hardy medium tree with good crops. There was one here but it went, as did others, in a gale. Pick lSept. Season Oct-Dec.

Lord Lambourne 7 MD 2 * JM

Laxton Bros. Beds. 1907. James Grieve X Worcester Pearmain. Named for RHS President. Shows the Worcester's strawberry flavour but with plenty of Grieves refreshingly sweet-sharp, juicy, crisp, flesh. It is a medium sized flat-round to mid-conical apple with a bright red flush and broken red stripes over a green-yellow to yellow ground. Widely grown in gardens and for local markets. It makes a medium sized tree and is partially tip-bearing. A good cropping variety to pick in mSept. Season lSept to Nov.

Meridian 7 MD

Marshalls, Wisbech exclusive c.2001 and said by them to be *'perhaps the perfect garden apple'*… Red Falstaff X Cox' Orange Pippin. Strong growing but compact… Bears heavy crops of large fruit. Pick m/lSept. Season Sept-Christmas.

Merton Beauty 7 MD 3

M. B. Crane, London, 1932. Ellison's Orange X Cox's Orange Pippin. Truly delicious if the strong flavour and scent of aniseed is liked. Rich, sweet, crisp, yet melting flesh. Short season for it becomes 'medicinal'; A good cropper. Pick eSept. Season Sept-Oct.

Minarette Registered Trade Mark. Ken Muir. Essex

Essentially a system for growing selected apple, pear and stone fruit cultivars. The tree is trained as a single cordon, before sale and comes with pruning instructions. **Falstaff** is the pollinator for all Minarette apples and the **Concorde** pear is self pollinating. The have the advantage of being suitable for growing in pots.

Mother (syn. American Mother) 6 MD 5

Massachusetts, 1844. It must be left on the tree to become, at best, exotic, aromatic, sweet, with juicy, soft, yellow flesh and with hints of vanilla, peardrops, balsam and spice – but in a poor year it collapses into flat, musty, sweetness. It was counted in Bunyard's 'Top Ten'. Found in old orchards and still available. The medium sized, medium to long-conical fruit has a deep red flush with broken red lines on a greenish yellow-to-yellow ground. It makes a medium sized upright tree, with erratic cropping. Pick lSept. Season Oct-Dec.

Norfolk Beauty 5 MC 2 Biennial

Mr. Allen a Head Gardener, Norwich, 1901. Warner's King X Waltham Abbey. A large apple, which cooks to a very well flavoured puree and needing little sugar. Very popular East Anglian garden tree. Pick eSept. Season Sept-Dec.

Norfolk Royal 6 MD 5

Wright's Nursery, Norfolk, c.1908. A rather greasy apple, which is becoming popular as 'pick-your-own', to be eaten crisp and sharp from the tree. It is of very striking appearance with white flesh and becomes crisp, sweet and juicy. The medium size conical, crowned fruit has a bright red flush and red stripes over a pale yellow ground with tiny dots. The tree has average vigour and crops well. **Norfolk Royal Russet** discovered Rev. Wright 1983 and introduced by Highfields Nursery is a better cultivar, more attractive, with a red cheek peeping through russet and with a rich, quite intense rich flavour. **Blackmoor Russet**, which I have, is either synonymous or very similar and is, in my opinion, a most worthwhile garden variety. Stocked by Blackmoor Estate, Hants. Pick eSept. Season Sept-Dec.

Orleans Reinette   7   LD   4   *

Orleans Reinette

France, 1776. When perfect it is nutty, sweet, aromatic, and firm, with rather dry pale cream flesh. Early fruit and windfalls diced; cook to keep their shape and it bakes well. In Bunyard's Top Six. A medium sized, flat-round to oblong fruit with a slight orange flush over much russet in netted patches and dots. It needs a warm site to develop flavour and a good crop. Pick mOct. Season Nov-Jan.

Peasegood's Nonesuch   4   M CD   3

Mrs. Peasegood, when a child in Grantham, c.1853-58. Once said to be one of the most handsome apples in cultivation, it cooks to a sweet, delicately flavoured puree and makes a very generous baked apple and is a favourite of ours. It is brisk, when eaten fresh and is good in salads. The large to very large round to mid-conical fruit has an orange-red flush with stripes over pale green becoming yellow, with a few russet spots. It makes an average but spreading tree which crops well but is prone to canker. Pick m-Sept. Season Sept-Dec.

Pitmaston Pine Apple   8   LD   3

Mr. White. Steward to Lord Fowley, Hereford, c.1785. Intensely pineapple-musk flavoured, rich, honeyed, sweet yet sharp and aromatic in a good year. The fruit is golden with fine netting and russet dots and is small and oblong-conical. Favoured by Hogg and Bunyard. Makes an average and spreading tree to pick in eOct. Season lOct-Dec.

Pixie   7   LD   4   *

RHS Wisley, 1947 *prob*. Either Cox or Sunset seedling. Aromatic, rich, sweet and acid. Harder and sharper than Cox. Smallish fruit but a good garden variety. Flat medium in shape the fruit is red flushed and striped over green to greenish-yellow ground. It makes a spreading tree of average vigour. Pick mOct. Season Dec-Mar.

Peasegood's Nonesuch

The Reverend W. Wilks

Also **Pixie Red Sport.**

Princesse 8 MD 3

New. France. Said to be a heavy cropping russet of good quality, less nutty than Egremont but easier to grow. Pick Sept. Season Nov.

Redsleeves 6 ED 3

D. Alston EMRS, Kent, 1956. Exeter Cross X Scab resistant seedling. Sweet, lightly aromatic, crisp, juicy flesh, but can be wooden and insipid. Both scab and mildew resistant. Pick lAug. Season Sept.

Red Windsor 6 MD 3 Registered Trademark.

Sport of Alkamene Hereford 1985. Said to be 'like a red Cox, but much easier and ideal for the garden'. Very compact growth. Pick Sept. Season Oct.

Reverend W. Wilks 3 EC 2

Messrs Vietch, 1904. Peasegood's Nonesuch X Ribston Pippin. Named for the then RHS Secretary and famed raiser of 'The Shirley Poppy'. A large mid-season apple. It becomes a compact tree with good disease resistance, which makes it most suitable for the small garden but it has a strong tendency toward biennial bearing. The fruit is whitish becoming primrose green to yellow with some broken stripes. It is sub-acid with a delicate aroma and cooks to a delicious pale yellow froth. Pick lAug-eSept. Season Sept-Oct.

Reverend W. Wilks

Ribston Pippin 7 LD 2 Triploid *

Sir Henry Goodricke. Believed seedling of a Rouen pip. c.1707. A most highly esteemed apple and still the most highly rated in Sweden. The original tree had appeared to die in 1835, but regrew to blow over in 1928 and died in 1932. A most beautifully flavoured apple, with intensely rich, honeyed, aromatic and juicy deep cream flesh. More acidity than Cox and not as delicate, but stronger with great depth and length. The most highly acclaimed apple of Victorian times. The fruit is round-conical to oblong-conical and somewhat ribbed with a brownish-orange flush and red stripes over gold, with some russet. Pick lSept-Oct. Season Oct-Jan.

Rosemary Russet 7 LD 3

Described Ronalds of Brentford,
1831. Sweet sharp, acid drop taste,
similar to Ashmead's Kernel but not
as sweet. One of Bunyard's 'Best late
sorts'. Remains to be a popular
garden apple and one, which we
like. The fruit is conical flat-sided
and ribbed and has an orange to
brownish-red flush over greenish
yellow/gold base. It makes an
upright tree, which crops well. Pick
e/mOct. Season Nov-Mar.

Rosemary Russet

St. Edmund's Pippin or Russet 8 MD 2 *

R. Harvey, Bury St Edmunds, 1875. Sweet, juicy, rich and densely textured pale
cream flesh. If picked too early it is hard and disappointing, but really ripe it has
been described as 'ambrosial'! A greatly valued garden variety. It has medium sized
fruit, which is flat-round to oblong-conical and has a silvery sheened, light russet
over greenish-yellow/gold ground. It bruises easily. The tree is of average vigour
and gives good crops. Pick mSept. Season lSept-Oct.

Saturn 4 ED SF

Completely resistant to scab and partially resistant to mildew. The fruit is glossy,
juicy and crisp. No details on taste or other qualities. Pick Sept. Said by
Marshall's to store until January.

Scrumptious 6 MD 3 Registered Trademark

Raised by Hugh Ermine and recently adopted by Marshall's. Round, red, crisp and
said to be 'of distinctive flavour and disease resistant'. Pick mSept. Season Oct.

Spartan 6 LD 3 *

British Columbia, 1926. Mackintosh X Yellow Newtown. Said to be, at its best,
perfumed with a vinous, strawberry/melon flavour, *'but if picked before it is coloured, it can
be tinny and bland with a tough skin'*. My experience of it is of having none of the
qualities, which I seek in an apple and with a celluloid skin filled with a wet-
spongy sweetness! It is a major Canadian apple with deep maroon skin and white
flesh. It gives heavy crops but is very prone to canker. Pick eOct. Season Nov-
Jan. Comm. Mar.

Sunset

Suntan

Sunset 7 MD 3 * SP

G. C. Addy, Kent, c.1918. Cox's Orange Pippin seedling. Like a small early Cox. Aromatic and intensely flavoured, robust and good but sharper than Cox, but much easier to grow. A well worth growing, garden cultivar, although prone to canker. Said to be too small for commerce, but we have found that by hand thinning in early July, the crop remains heavy enough but with small-medium fruits. The fruit has a diffuse orange flush and many red stripes over gold with russet patches. Pick l-Sept. Season Oct-Dec. Sunset Sport is more highly coloured.

Suntan 7 LD 5 Triploid *

H. M. Tydeman EMRS, Kent, 1956. Cox's Orange Pippin X Court Pendu Plat. Handsome, robustly aromatic, rich sweet and with much pineapple acidity but extremely sharp if eaten too soon. It is said to be a good cropper, but we have found it to be light, yet worthwhile. It may be that we do not have enough late flowering cultivars for pollination. It makes a spreading tree and is prone to bitter pit and canker. The medium sized fruit is flat-round bright orange-red with red stripes over gold. Pick e/mOct. Season Nov-Feb.

Tom Putt 3 E M C Cyder & D 3

Either Rev. T. Putt, Dorset or T. Putt, Barrister, Devon. Late 1700s. Not remarkably good for other than stewing but can be a sharp eater or a cyderapple. The cyder is thin and used for blending. The fruit is large and bright red flushed. It crops well and is resistant to scab. Pick eSept. Season Sept-Nov. **Sidney Strake** is less highly coloured sport.

Tydeman's Late Orange 7 LD 4

H. M. Tydeman EMRS, Kent, 1930. Laxton's Superb X Cox's Orange Pippin. Intensely rich and aromatic in Dec, sharper and stronger than Cox. Sweetens by March to be only lightly aromatic, but still good. We find it to be much easier to grow than Cox. The fruit is medium to small, conical to round-conical and has a dark purplish-red flush, with darker red stripes over greenish-yellow/yellow ground. It has heavy crops on whippy growth, like Superb. Pick mOct. Season Dec-Apr.

Tydeman's Late Orange

Warner's King   1   LC   2   Triploid

Orig King Apple, Warner, late 1700s. Renamed Thos. Rivers, Nurseryman. Also known as Killick's Apple in Kent and in the North as T. Fish (A Head Gardener) Cooks to a strongly flavoured, sharp puree, but never as sharp as Bramley. It was a favourite of the Victorians and once a principal Market apple, but it is too big and bruises too easily for supermarkets. It was widely grown as an arbour or tunnel tree, because of its very pretty flowers and remains to be a good garden tree. The fruit is very large, flat-round or conical and is pale green becoming pale yellow. The crop is heavy, but prone to bitter pit. Pick lSept. Season Sept-Dec.

William Crump   6/7   LD   5   *

Claimed by Carless, foreman Rowe's Nursery but shown to be a Cox's Orange Pippin X Worcester Pearmain seedling raised by the distinguished fruitman William Crump Head Gardener, Madresfield Court. Intense aromatic flavour, rich, sweet and with much pineapple acidity in Nov. Mellows to be more Cox-like. The fruit has a bright orange-red flush with red strips over green-yellow/yellow ground with much russet as dots netting and patches. The tree is upright and the crop good. Pick mOct. Season Dec-Feb.

Winter Gem   6   L   D   3

H. Ermen, Kent, c.1985. A newish cultivar, said to be a strongly growing, heavy cropping and richly flavoured, aromatic, pink flushed apple of exceptional quality, which is a 'winner at flavour competitions'. (Frank Matthews, 'Growing Trees for Life', 1901-2001, ex Brogdale)

Worcester Pearmain   6   ED   3   SP

Mr. Hale, Market Gardener, Worc, 1873. (Prob. Devonshire Quarrenden X) Of the brightest red, extremely sweet and markedly strawberry flavoured. (…'Boiled sweets and synthetic pear juice' Morton Shand). Its almond to white blossom made it very popular as a decorative planting around 1900. It must not be picked until it is perfectly ripe or it is chewy and insipid. Picked when completely ripe and eaten straight from the tree, it is pleasant enough but quickly cloys. It makes pleasant cyder if it is helped to start fermenting by the addition of some sharp apples and it blends well to attenuate the acidity of the later 'culinary' cyders (Bramley). Harvest and eat m/lSept.

Many of these cultivars are available, thanks only to organisations, such as Brogdale and the few nurserymen who are dedicated to preserving the English Apple and of course, discerning kitchen gardeners. The great hybridising nurseries, such as Laxtons', are gone and built-over and few of the more recent cultivars have much to commend them to the connoisseur. One or two supermarkets 'support' English Apples, either by sponsoring 'Apple Days' or by 'adopting' a variety, but they must be encouraged to do much more by a 'connoisseur' clientele. Cox's, Russets and Bramley's seem safe for the present… If supermarkets are to do more than boast of giving 'More choice' and 'Supporting British', and then they must behave as did the Real fruiterers whom they replaced and offer home grown varieties in season.

1,936 Brogdale Apples

Cyder Apples

Cyderapples are classified differently from dessert and culinary varieties and the varieties are described as flowering – (E)arly, (M)id-season or (L)ate.

And in four main groupings – Sharps, Bittersharps, Bittersweets and Sweets and these may be prefixed by –Medium, Full or Mild.

In the most general of terms, Sharps have the least tannins, (as low as 1 gram/litre) and the most acidity (as high as10 grams/litre), whilst Bitters may have only 1 gram/litre acid and up to 7 grams/litre of tannins.

Most cyders are fermented from a blend of varieties, but some, which are styled 'Vintage', are considered to possess all the qualities required for a 'Single Variety Vintage Cyder'. My selection is based upon the commonest cultivars, which have been recommended by The Long Ashton Research Station as 'Vintage'. Average juice sugar content is shown in °Oechsle. (See Appendices), together with average acid and tannins in grams/litre.

Bramley's Seedling   Considered as Full Sharp   45°   Acid 8+g/l   Little Tannin

It is a useful acid carrier in blending but should not be considered as a 'Vintage' variety.

Brown's Apple   late-M   Full Sharp   48°   Acid 6.7g/l   Tannin 1.2g/l

Slow to start but makes a vigorous tree, with some resistance to scab but susceptible to mildew and canker and with a strong tendency to being biennial. Very widely planted in Devon and Somerset, where it can produce huge crops and high quality clean, sharp and aromatic cyder… and it bakes well. Falls in late Oct.

Bulmer's Foxwhelp   E/M   Med. Bittersharp   53°   Acid   5.5g/l   Tannins 2.4g/l

Makes a robust, healthy tree. The cropping is a little irregular, but the fruit is usually high in sugars and the cyder full bodied. The fruit will fall from mid Oct.

Crabapples and decorative cultivars.

Species, for examples *Malus zumi*, *M.baccata*, *M.Tschonoskii*, hedgerow crabs and decorative cultivars such as John Downie and Golden Hornet, which can have Oechsle levels of up to 60°, will enhance home cyders and may be assumed to behave as bittersweets. Some home cyder makers use them alone. We have a number of species and domesticated crabs and they all go into <u>blended</u> cyders.

True crabs may be distinguished from domestic escapes by their new growth being clear of 'wool' or down.

Dabinett   Late M   Med. Bittersweet   57°
Acid 1.8g/l   Tannins 2.9g/l

A rounded and spreading tree, which appears to require generous potash availability. It is a precocious and regular bearer with above average sugar content. Its cyder is of above average vintage

Dabinett

quality, full bodied and astringent. My tree has had regularly good crops since it came into bearing. Fruit falls Oct-Nov.

Harry Master's Jersey
Late-Mid Full Bittersweet   56° Acid 2g/l   Tannins 3.2g/l

A compact small tree, which gives good annual crops. The fruit falls in Oct-Nov and sometimes needs prompt milling. It is considered to make cyder of merit.

Michelin M Med. Bittersweet 50°   Acid 2.3g/l Tannins 2.3g/l

Not a 'Vintage' variety but included because of its reliability and for being a most used blending variety of high quality. It is a moderately growing tree with a stiff upright habit. Produces annually and can be three weeks in falling from mid to late Oct. Young trees are prone to mildew, and canker, but not especially to crown rot.

Sweet Alford M Sweet 52° Acid 2.2g/l Tannins 1.5g/l

One of the most valued all-round vintage varieties. Moderately strong growing and can be a large tree. The cropping is moderate but annual and it is a tip-bearer. The sugar content and juice yield are above average and the fruit falls from late Oct. Very prone to scab.

Sweet Coppin M Sweet JS 52° Acid 2g/l Tannins 1.4g/l

A moderate to strongly growing tree, which crops well, if with a biennial tendency. The sugar content is good and with no astringency. A useful vintage variety falling from late Oct-Nov.

Sweet Coppin

Tom Putt M Mild Sharp 52° Acid 6.5g/l Tannins 1.3g/l

Not in any way a 'vintage' variety, but useful (See elsewhere). We had a tree on MM106 but it fell to collar rot, a not uncommon failing with MM106 and we did not feel it to be worth replacing. Unblended, it made a clean, but thin, dry sharp cyder and was improved by blending with such as Worcester Pearmain. Greatly loved by codling moth! Drops in August and needs to be processed quickly.

Yarlington Mill Jersey

Mixed apples for cyder and a few Medlars
(Yarlington Mill in foreground)

Malus Zumi

Yarlington Mill Jersey
M   Mild Bittersweet   52°
Acids 2.2g/l   Tannins 3.2g/l

Makes moderate to good growth with a
tendency towards a drooping habit and
has very pretty flowers. It can become
biennial if neglected. My tree has
maintained a reasonable annual cropping,
to date. It is considered to be a superior
all-round variety and its very brightly
coloured fruit fall from early November.
The cyder has a good aroma and flavour.

Yarlington Mill

Pears

The few pear cultivars, which are offered in present day commerce, are chosen for
shelf-life and bruise resistance and are unlikely to be of premier eating quality or
to have been picked at an optimum time. If a pear is to be savoured at its most
meltingly sublime, then it is likely to be one which you have grown yourself and
watched to be eaten when 'just right!' – It is said… *'Pears, when really ready, are best
eaten in the bath!'* The story goes that you plant pears for your heirs, but, in fact, a
pear on Quince may fruit quite well from the second year after planting.

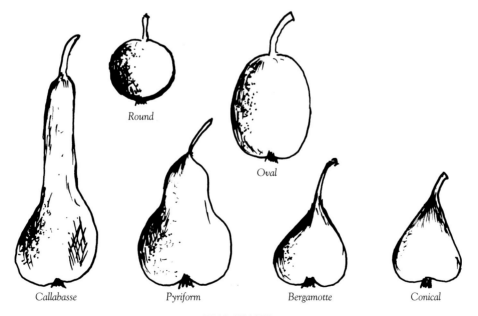

Round

Oval

Callabasse   *Pyriform*   *Bergamotte*   *Conical*

PEAR SHAPES

A selection of pears in a variety of shapes

Pears flower from late March and may need a long season to reach perfection. Few are suitable for colder parts of UK and do best with some protection, particularly against wind and frost. My selection is based on Jim Arbury's 'Pears'.

All but the culinary Catillac are dessert varieties, but when firm, all may be used as culinary fruit.

Most pears, like apples, are diploid and are compatible with any other in their group or neighbouring groups. There are four pollination groups (A, B, C, D). One or two cultivars are triploid, producing no useful pollen and require two other compatible cultivars as do one or two 'male sterile' diploids (none chosen). There are a few tetraploids and these are treated, as if diploids.

Beth (D)

H. M. Tydeman EMRS, 1938. A compact and reliable garden variety, which can ripen in the North. It has conical to short-conical fruit, which are smooth, pale green to pale yellow fruit with russet. Pick in late August and eat in early to mid-Sept.

Beurré Hardy (C)

M. Bonnet, Boulogne c.1820. A vigorous, upright tree with reliably good cropping. A good quality pear, which had a commercial following until quite recently. We used to buy it locally until the orchard became a housing estate. It is an excellent garden cultivar with sweet buttery 'rose-water' flavoured flesh. Its medium to large, round-conical to pyriform fruit are rough and light green covered with russet. The form **Red Buerré Hardy** differs only in being about 50% red flushed. Pick mSept. Season October.

Catillac (D) Triploid

One of the oldest in cultivation it dates to before 1665. May have origin in the Gironde. It requires slow cooking for up to two hours to become attractively pale-pink and well flavoured. It is the best cooking pear and will thrive in the North and is superior to all dessert pears for cooking. It is a large bergamotte shaped fruit with smooth lumpy, skin, which is dull green becoming yellow. Pick mOct. Season Jan-Apr.

Concord (C)

EMRS, Kent, 1977. Doyenne du Comice X Conference. A very good and compact garden tree which crops regularly and heavily. The fruit has pale yellow, melting flesh with a buttery texture and a mild, but pleasant flavour. It is medium to large, pyriform to calabasse and has pale green to yellow skin, heavy gold-brown russetting. Pick late September. Season Oct-Nov.

Conference (C)

Rivers, Nurserymen, Herts. Exhibited at the National Pear Conference 1885. It is most reliable and will set and ripen without a pollinator. The flavour is good, when ripe, but supermarkets do persist in selling it whilst it is rock hard. If you buy it from a supermarket, then store it until a trace of pear scent is noticed. It is the most grown pear in Britain. The fruit is pyriform to calabasse and the yellowish green, roughish skin, has, sometimes, a pinkish flush. Pick late September. Season Oct-Nov.

Doyenne du Comice (D)

Comice Horicole, Angers, before 1849. In the opinion of many, by far the finest of pears, but one which must have a warm site. Ours is as a single cordon on a south-facing wall. We eat this delightful cultivar in High Suffolk between **mid and late** November#. The story goes that you should not bite into a Comice until the juice runs to your elbow! The fruit is medium to large and pyriform to bergamotte, pale green becoming pale yellow, sometimes with a red flush. There are a number of red sports. Pick early October. Season mid-Oct to mid-Nov#.

Glou Morceau (D)

Abbé Hardenpont, pioneer pear breeder, c.1750. Introduced into England 1820. An excellent and reliable pear which needs a warm wall and a good summer to be at its finest. It is oval to pyriform with pale green skin, which becomes pale yellowish-green. The flesh is finely textured, melting and juicy and strongly pear flavoured.

Doyenne du Comice

Josephine de Malines

Goldember (D)

A new cultivar, presently exclusive to Marshalls of Wisbech. It is said to be a precocious and reliable bearer of golden and fragrantly juicy fruit of up to 8oz (250g). Pick early October. Season More than one month if kept cool.

Jargonelle (C) Triploid

Mentioned by Parkinson in 1629 but older. Hardy, long-lived and grown all over the UK. It is best, as a bush because it is a partial tip bearer. It quickly rots from the core and so timing is of the essence. It is a medium sized long-conical to pyriform fruit, with generally smooth skin, with rough russet patches and green to yellowish green in colour. It has pale yellow flesh, tender and juicy with a slightly musky flavour. Cooks well. Pick early-mid August. Season mid-late August.

Josephine de Malines (C)

Major Esperon, Malines, Belgium and named for his wife. 1830. A weak grower, which is best on Quince A and in a sheltered position. There is a tendency toward tip-bearing and so it is not the best candidate for wall training, but we do have it on a south-facing wall, because we have no better site. It has good resistance to scab. Ours is ready, usually, in late January and varies from good to fair in flavour with melting, very sweet flesh. The fruit is small and bergamotte to short-conical. The skin is smooth to rough where russetted and pale green turning to yellowish green as it ripens. Pick late Oct. Season January-February.

Louise Bonne de Jersey (B)

M. Longueval, Normandy, 1780. A very heavy cropping cultivar, which sometimes needs fruit thinning and will ripen in the north. A well flavoured garden pear of moderate vigour. It is a small to medium sized pear with pale green turning to yellowish green skin with sometimes russet dots on a red flush. Pick mid to late September. Season October.

Merton Pride® Triploid

John Innes Hort Inst, Merton, 1941. Glou Morceau X Double William's. A splendid variety for the garden and very juicy. It is a very strong grower and best on Quince C. It has a large fruit, which is pyriform to conical with a green becoming yellow skin. The flesh is cream-white – softly melting, very sweet, juicy and most pear-flavoured. Pick September. Season mid to late September.

Nouveau Poiteau (D)

Van Mons, Belgium, 1827. A good garden cultivar with heavy and reliable crops.

It has oval-pyriform fruit, which are green. turning pale green. Some fruit is heavily russetted and some is bare. It is sweet, melting, juicy and well flavoured. Recommended for northern growing. Pick early to mid October. Season November.

Packham's Triumph   (B)

C. H. Packham, Australia, 1896. Uvedale's St. Germain X William's Bon Chrétien. A good and reliable pear both commercially and for the garden. It does not like cold winds and we have found that it fails after a cold windy spring, even when having flowered well. It has very bumpy pyriform fruit, which is bright green becoming pale yellow. The flesh is finely textured, pale yellow, juicy and musky. Pick late Sept. Season Oct-Nov.

Pitmaston Duchess   (D)   Triploid

J. Williams, Pitmaston, 1841. A very vigorous grower, best on Quince A and is a good cultivar for the north. Of very high quality it has melting, yellowish-white, juicy, flesh. The fruit is very large, sometimes up to 500g, long-conical to pyriform with light green changing to pale yellow with a red flush. It is, unfortunately, prone to scab. Pick mid-late Sept. Season October.

Rocha   (D)

A Portuguese pear, which crops reliably and well here. It keeps quite well and is a standard 'handsome but hard' supermarket pear. Grown to be picked in late September, it may be kept for a little time in the fridge and eaten as it becomes juicy and sweet.

Santa Maria   (D)

A small fruited variety, but with sweet and buttery flesh. A reliable and regular bearer to pick and eat in August.

Verdi   (D)

A new variety bred from Doyenne du Comice. The fruits have a reddish tinge and are said to be fine textured, very juicy, sweet and aromatic. Reported as being a reliably regular cropper with fruits of up to 1lb (500g). Pick early October. Season... no other details.

Williams' Bon Chrétien   (C)

Mr. Wheeler, Schoolmaster, Berks, before 1770 and given to a nurseryman R. Williams. Liked very much in France it was renamed after St. William Bon

Pyrus sp. (Seed collected Mosel 1986)

Chrétien, an Italian holy-man who was dubbed 'Bon Chrétien' because, when asked by a king to confirm his assumed immortality had preferred to tell the truth. 'That all, kings and subjects alike are made mortal by God' and had been invited to extend his own mortality by fleeing Italy, with haste! It was first grown in the USA, at the turn of the 18th. Century by Mr. Carter, Massachusetts. The land passed to Mr. Bartlett who went on to found the tinned pear industry with 'Bartlett' pears, unaware, apparently, of its true identity. It is an easy, reliable and good cropping pear but very prone to scab, which excludes growing it in the west. It rots very quickly from the core if picking is left too late. The fruit is uneven, pyriform and pale green becoming bright yellow as it ripens. It is a very pleasant pear when perfect, with an interesting history, but we keep ours, only because it is a good pollinator for Doyenne Du Comice. Pick early September. Season mid-late September.

Winter Nelis   (D)

J-C Nelis Malines, c.1800, introduced UK 1818. A weak grower, which is best on Quince A. It is a reliable cropper but can need fruit thinning or the size suffers. The fruit is pale green, juicy and well flavoured. It has small to medium sized fruit which is round-conical and has pale green becoming yellowish green skin covered in russet spots and patches. Pick late October. Season December to January.

If a pear is to be savoured at its best then it must be picked at the right time and stored cool, resting on its base and separate, until it is completely ready. It is said of some connoisseurs that they will sit and watch and sniff, through the night if necessary, awaiting the perfect moment! Farm shops, rather than supermarkets, are the most likely to respond to any connoisseur-demand.

All the above cultivars will juice, but none are of much use for perry, although

Long Ashton's 'Perry Pears' suggests that they may make acceptable beverage perry *'if it is to be consumed in areas which have no perry tradition!'* Any substandard eating pears, which I have, go in with cyder.

Perry Pears

Perrypears, like cyderapples, are too tannic to be eaten, but they will cook well. Unlike cyderapples they cannot be blended without risk of forming immovable tannic-pectic hazes. They do not share a major acid, some having mostly malic acid and others citric acid, some are low in acidity and others high. They have complex and numerous tannins and some have a proportion of higher unfermentable sugars and they have different storage times prior to milling. It is more difficult to make good perry than good cyder, but this will be dealt with in a later chapter. Another complication is that some perrypears are not compatible with quince and need to be double-grafted – usually on Buerré Hardy on Quince – but most do not. Double-grafted trees will cost more, but a specialist raiser will have made the decision to double-graft from experience.

My recommendations are based upon Long Ashton's first choice cultivars and a couple of others, which I have grown.

The **Flowering Groups** are given as being… Early, Mid, Late or Very Late (1, 2, 3 or 4).

The Harvest Times are, for example September, Early October, Late October and November. And maturing time before milling is in weeks.

For Example: **Brandy** 2/3 **E-LO** Up to 4.

Barnet 3 **LO** Variable av. 3

A medium to large compact tree of some 30 feet (9m) spread having large limbs and obvious spurs. It has a tendency toward biennial bearing but is of great merit, with resistance to scab. It was much propagated and distributed by Long Ashton. The gravity is 52°Oe, the acidity low (2.8g/l) and low tannin (0.9g/l). The perry is light, pleasant and of average quality.

Blakeney Red 2 **LE-MO** 1

Makes a medium to large tree with acute crotches and of some 40-50 feet (15m) of canopy. Young trees have numerous upright limbs, which, eventually, fuse. It crops heavily with a gravity of 56°Oe, acid 4.2g/l and 1.3… making a medium acid, medium tannin perry of pleasant average quality, when milled at the right time.

Barnet

Blakeney Red

Brandy

Butt

67

Brandy 2/3 **E-LO** Up to 4

A small to medium spreading tree with a canopy of about 20 feet (6m) having good angled crotches. Gives good crops but has a tendency toward being biennial. It makes medium acid, low tannin perry, somewhat bland but aromatic, dark in colour and of average quality. The expected sugar content rises, dramatically, with age – young trees averaging 46° Oechsle and older ones 69°. The acid and tannin rises too, to 4.4g/l and 1.2g/l respectively. My own tree is yet young and gives only light crops to date, which have gone into blended cyder.

Brown Bess 2 **LO** 4

Makes a medium to large tree of upright habit with narrow angled crotches with a canopy of about 15metres. Originally a culinary pear and a good bearer. Sugars 55°Oe and of medium acid (5.5g/l) and is considered as having a 'high citric' content, low tannin (1g/l), making average to good perry.

Butt 2/3 **LN** 4-10

Makes a spreading large tree with narrow angles and drooping boughs covering about 10 metres. It crops heavily but with a strong biennial habit. It is popular and with it goes the saying 'Gather your Butts one year, mill them the next, and drink the year after'… on account of its long milling period and the cultivar's resistance to rotting after the fall. Gravity 56°. Acidity med/high 5.4g/l, high tannin 5.2g/l making an astringent, fruity perry of medium to high quality. This perry precipitates tannin during storage.

Gin 2/3 **MO** 3-5

A medium sized slightly spreading tree with narrow crotches with high resistance to scab and canker, which has a canopy of around 30 feet (9m). It crops very well but shows a biennial tendency.

The fruit keeps well and juices to a gravity of 52°Oe with medium acid and acidity (4.2g/l and 1.5g/l).

Gin is considered to have a relatively high citric acid content. The perry is of average to good quality.

Hendre Huffcap 1 **EO** 2

A medium to large tree of 10-15 metres spread with few long upright limbs from wide angled crotches which are prone to breaking if the crop is too large. The crop is very easily shaken down. There are few trees left in cultivation, but Long Ashton, believe that its many good characteristics make it worthy of more

Hendre Huffcap

Moorcroft

Oldfield

Yellow Huffcap

Perry pears maturing
(Left: Oldfield. Right: Hendre Huffcap)

propagating.

The gravity is 59°Oe, its acidity low/medium (3.7g/l) and with low tannin (0.8g/l). It makes very pleasant perry of good to vintage quality. I have bought its fruit from Brogdale over the past few years and have been very pleased with its perries.

Judge Amphlett   1   LS-EO   0-1

A tree with a spread of around 30 feet (9m) with a strong central leader. A somewhat twiggy habit and one of the heaviest cropping varieties. The gravity is 53°Oe and the perry is light and of average quality. It is of medium acid and low tannin (4.3g/l and 0.9g/l).

Moorcroft   2   M-LS   Immediately

A large tree with a large canopy (15m) and with a small number of acutely angled limbs. It is a widely grown variety despite its having little resistance to scab. The gravity of the must is high (66°Oe). With medium acidity and tannin (5g/l and 1.7g/l) it makes generally good to excellent quality perry, but it must be processed as it is picked.

Oldfield   3   M-LS   3-60

Makes a small to medium tree, which is very prone to canker, and healthy trees are few. Nevertheless it is of high repute and produces vintage quality perry wherever it is clean. East Anglia has no perry tradition and my Oldfield is yet young. Its tiny crops are a bonus for it was planted with no more than hope – for someone! The must weight is 65°Oe with medium to high acid and medium tannin (7.3g/l and 1.5g/l). It is considered to have a high citric acid content.

Species Pears   ?

The Kelts used wild pears for perry making, long before there were named cultivars and retained trees, which gave the best results – a practice, which resulted in 'cultivars'. Many of the commoner perry cultivars originated as single farm discoveries. Our several 'Mosel' wild pears (Most probably *P.communis/nivalis X*), were grown from seeds collected near Cochem in 1986. They are a splendid sight in flower and one fruited for the first time last year (2001). The fruit was small and hard and

Pear 'Mosel' sp.

bitter, like a Suffolk 'I-ron' pear. There were too few to trial and so they went in with the cyder. The flourish is again a delight this year and my hopes are high!

I raise seedlings every year from crabs, cyderapples and perrypears and allow nature to choose the survivors, which are labelled to take their chances in the field.

Thorn   2   M-LS   up to 1

A very old variety (pre-1676), which makes a small tree of upright habit and gives heavy crops. It is much liked for its compact habit and was, originally, a culinary pear. The gravity is 62°Oe and makes medium acid and low tannin (5.7g/l and 1g/l) perry of average to good quality.

Yellow Huffcap   1   E   up to 1

A large tree with large spreading limbs and twiggy branches. It crops heavily if with a tendency to being biennial. It is widely planted and lauded for the quality of its perry. It is usually double grafted. My own tree is not yet in bearing. The must gravity is 64° Oechsle. It makes medium to high acidity (6.2g/l), low tannin (1g/l) and full flavoured, fruity, perry of consistently high to excellent quality.

Perrypear cultivars exist for far longer than apple cultivars and each tree is also longer lived and some may approach 500 years.

Other Pomes

Hawberries (*Crataegus sp.*) The Common Hawthorn (*C.monogyna*) and May (*C.orientalis (oxyacantha)*) – and childhood's 'Bread and Cheese', when the opening leaf buds are nibbled with flavoured imagination! All hawberries can be used to make preserves and sauces and have good Vitamin C content. They remain of interest to latter day hunter-gatherers – 'hedgerow cooks'! The Cockspur Thorn (*C.crus-galli*) has large 'spurs' and was once a source for the needles of those Edwardian clockwork gramophones with huge papier-mâché horns. It is well worth growing if for no other than ornament, for its bright pillar-box red fruit hang until well after Christmas.

The pretty purple anthered Azarole (*C.azarolus*) is cultivated in Mediterranean countries for its 1" (2.5cm) red, orange or yellow fruits, which taste very much like apple. They are eaten from the hand or made into jelly or 'cyder'. The Mexican Manzanilla (*C.pubescen*) was an American Indian staple. The fruit is 2" (5cm) in diameter and yellow. The Mississippi Hawberry (*C.coccinioides*) has bright red 1cm berries, which are very juicy. <u>All these Hawberries</u> are perfectly hardy and decorative.

Medlar (*Mespilus germanica*) is native to Iran and was quite likely to have come here with the Phonecians or other early traders. It was once much more commonly grown than it is now and was prized in Elizabethan cuisine. It is self-fertile and the only species. It is a close relative of the Pear and its fruit looks like a small flattened and russetted pear. Its large calyx has made it the butt for ribaldry and remains 'cul de chien' – dog's arse – in rural France. I think it to be one of those fruits, which, if you take to it as a child, you love it forever. It is very tannic and needs to be 'bletted', that is to say, part rotted, before it can be eaten. Ours, either stay on the tree for the birds, or go into the cyder mix as they fall, but a friend, now sadly gone, used to take the crop for dessert and to make jelly. The ancient belief that Medlar 'quiets the heated stomach' was upheld by recent scientific enquiry, when it was found to have pectins, sugars, tannins and gums in a perfect combination for soothing indigestion. A 17th Century herbal considers… *'There is no better than Old Saturn's Fruit to strengthen an old man's retentive faculty and thereby stay his wife from a-gadding'*… The tree is slow growing, twisting and drooping of habit and well worth having for its architectural form, its beautiful flowering and its striking autumn colours, whether the fruit is to be harvested or not.

It dislikes cold wind and resents hard pruning, which it punishes by growing atypically vertical water-wood… best left to get on with it! The most easily found varieties are 'Nottingham', a slow growing small tree with yellowish-brown russetted 1" (2.5cm) fruit and 'Dutch', with 2.5" (6cm) greyish-green russet fruit.

Nottingham is the better flavoured... according to medlar connoisseurs.

Quince (*Cydonia oblonga*) is also monotypic. The Japanese Quince (*Chaenomeles japonica var*), which is spiny and the Chinese Quince (*Pseudocydonia sinensis var*), which is not, are small shrubby relatives, with very pretty flowers and similar but inferior fruits. It is native to Iran and Anatolia but was well known to the early Mediterranean peoples. Our name derives from '(The Apple of) Kydonia' through the Langue d'Oc 'cydonia' and the French 'coings'. It once grew wild in the southern counties when the fruit was (and is still) made into a rich and refreshing wine and it may be found, yet, in ancient hedges. Quinces can reach 20' (6m) and make bushy topped trees. They are self-fertile and tip bearing, love the sun and hate wind. Quince is, usually, twiggy and seldom needs attention, but any pruning out of spent branches should be done in winter. The showy pink-white flowers burst in late May and become rich yellow pear shaped fruits. A delicious aroma around the tree in October signals harvest-time, but the fruit can hang for admiration, long after the leaves have gone. One quince will scent a room and in the days before central heating, quince sweetened the linen chest and wardrobe and sock-drawers. The hard fruit will keep for a couple of months if kept cool. It may be made into jam and jelly and is prized in France for making the preserve Cotignac. In the ratio of one to twelve, quinces enhance apple tarts or stewed apple most wonderfully.

Marmelo, (Portuguese for Quince) is the root of our word 'marmalade'. Quince deserves to be grown much more widely than it is, for it is an easy subject which both, enhances the garden and broadens our cuisine. The most easily sourced varieties are... The Serbian 'Bereczki 'and the similar 'Vranja', which are both of excellent quality... the American, 'Meech's Prolific', which has consistently high yields and 'Portugal', an early ripener which turns a deeper colour than others when cooked, is said to be the very best culinary variety.

Sorb Apples (*Sorbus spp.*) of which there are about 100, are, broadly, Whitebeams (example *S.aria*), Service Trees and Mountain Ashes or Rowans. (Examples: *S.aucuparia, S.domestica, S.hupihensis*)... Whitebeams and Service Trees are used, most usually, as ornamentals and are little known here for their edible fruits, which, are used in some countries to make 'cyders', jams, jellies and liqueurs. If firm, sorbs make jellies and if ripe and bletted, liqueurs. The Wild Service Tree Sorbus torminalis, is an even less known striking ornamental with edible fruit. All sorbapples were very popular in the great gardens, the Wild Service Tree being the fussiest, growing mostly in the south. Ours grows slowly and is not completely happy in East Anglia. Rowans and Whitebeams are much more at home.

Many years ago, when were in New York staying with my brother and sister-in-law, we saw The Russian Georgian State Dance Group present traditional dances, gliding as though on castors. In one of the dances the ladies carried fruiting Sorbus branches and wove in and out and around the men in a most unforgettably sensuous, 'pome' fertility dance.

Grafting Stocks

Apple and pear cultivars are grown on rootstocks, which have been chosen for their influence on the cultivars' growth and fruiting habits. (See drawing)

There are upwards of 20 apple stocks and 10 pear stocks in use, but only those which are commonly used for garden trees are included in my selection and are, for apples – the East Malling and Merton-Malling clones and for pears Quince A and C. Other pomes are left on their own roots or as cultivars, are grafted on quince, pear or hawthorn.

Apples

M2 (Doucin Paradise) is a vigorous stock and will result in a 12' (3.5m) tree in a wide variety of soils. It is happy to be grassed down.

M9 (Jaune de Metz) is the most used dwarfing stock. It promotes precocious and regular cropping and larger fruit size and it is very resistant to collar rot (*Phytophthera cactorium*). If it is used it is imperative that the tree is given a stout stake throughout its lifetime, because of the poor anchorage given by M9. It must be pruned adequately and regularly and because of the limited root system, it will, most probably need irrigation.

M25 (Northern Spy X M2) is a very vigorous stock and will drive a tree to at least 15' (4.5m). It is best if the need is for a full standard tree.

M26 (M16 X M9) is a semi-dwarfing stock and is most often used on such naturally strong growers as Bramley's Seedling and it is very resistant to cold. It is liable to producing unwanted growth around the join, which can encourage entry of disease if not cut off as it appears. The recommendation when using this stock is to plant with the join barely above ground level.

M27 (M15 X M9) is a fully dwarfing clone and it is only suitable for use in highly productive land, kept weed-free and irrigated and its trees must have permanent staking. It is preferable to **M26** for garden patio and tub planting.

MM106 (Northern Spy X M1) is, probably, the most used rootstock. It is semi-vigorous on rich soils but less so on poorer soils. The major disadvantage is its proneness to collar rot and so it is best avoided on heavy soils. On the whole it is the best for gardeners who expect to grass down their fruit.

MM111 (Northern Spy X (Northern Spy X M2)) is more vigorous than MM106, but better for drier land. It needs a careful pruning regime.

Pears

All pears in Britain, other than Asian Pears are on East Malling clonal Quince (*Cydonia oblonga*) rootstocks. Asian Pears are on cloned seedling Asian Pear (*Pyrus pyrifolia*).

Quince A is used if a larger tree is required, but **Quince C** is the most used in orchard planting. Some pear cultivars are uncomfortable or incompatible when grafted directly onto Quince. For instance Conference is prone to 'Pear decline' (Parry's disease) and the search continues for a suitable *Pyrus* alternative.

William's Bon Chrétien is incompatible with quince and is double grafted with, usually, Buerré Hardy as the intergraft.

Comprehensive lists of cultivars of apples and pears will be found in The Book of Apples, Cider and Juice Apples, The English Apple, Pears, Perry Pears and A Somerset Pomona.

… *'God never wrought miracle to convince atheists, for his ordinary works confound them'*…
Roger Bacon 1561-1626

CHAPTER TWO SUMMARY

★ The Modern English apple began in 1825 with Cox's Orange Pippin.

★ Cox's Orange Pippin, Ribston's Pippin, Blenheim Orange and Bramley's Seedling remain the measures for all other cultivars.

★ Supermarkets select apples and pears for shelf life, resistance to long transportation and eye appeal.

★ Apples and pears cease to have social or seasonal significance.

★ Descriptions of more than 100 apples, pears and other pomes and grafting stocks.

★ Many cultivars owe their continued existence to enthusiastic nurserymen, collections and kitchen gardeners.

★ The Quince, the Medlar and other pomes deserve to be more widely cultivated… for form, flower and cuisine.

★ Choice of grafting stock determines vigour and ultimate size.

Cultivation

Site and Planting

If an apple or pear is to fruit regularly and successfully, then it must have a sunny site and be out of cold spring winds. A south-facing wall is said to give 1°F of frost protection for every 1' of height. (1.5°C/m) and most commercial orchards will have a poplar or alder hedge on, at least the 'cold' boundary.

Apples will be happy in a wide variety of soil types, so long as they have adequate depth for their root system and free drainage. Shallow soils can become arid very quickly and easily and a drought-damaged root system will never recover, fully. Waterlogged soil will have a similarly detrimental effect.

Pears are equally, if not more requiring of shelter, for they flower earlier, but they will tolerate poorer soils than the apple. Marshall, reporting on Perry Pears in 1789, said that he had seen them *'Flourishing on blue clay, such as would support no other herbage than wood-fescue'*, but it is much better to assume their needs as approaching, but of being less demanding than, those of the apple. Neither likes dry chalky soils.

Planting

Container grown trees may be planted at any time of the year, but it is my opinion that it is best to buy bare rooted feathered maidens or 2-3 year trees, from specialist growers and to plant at some frost-free time, between October and March.

The site should be free from perennial weed and the planting holes prepared immediately before planting. Trees should be planted at the distances, which are recommended for particular rooting stocks.

The planting hole must be large enough to contain the spread roots and deep enough for the young tree to be planted at <u>the same depth</u> as when it was in the nursery's bed.

Drive a permanent stake or a stout temporary cane into the hole before planting, (all dwarf trees and spindletrees will require a stake for their entire lives.) and

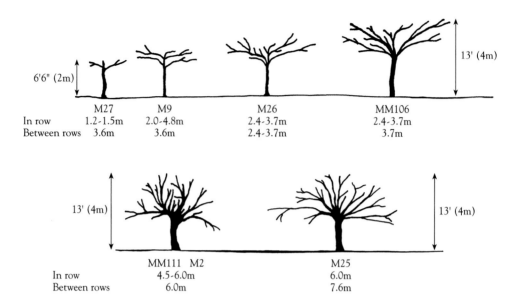

	M27	M9	M26	MM106
In row	1.2-1.5m	2.0-4.8m	2.4-3.7m	2.4-3.7m
Between rows	3.6m	3.6m	2.4-3.7m	3.7m

	MM111 M2	M25
In row	4.5-6.0m	6.0m
Between rows	6.0m	7.6m

EFFECTS OF DIFFERENT ROOTSTOCKS

sprinkle a small handful of bone meal and fork the soil below the bed for the roots, before laying-in the tree; inverting any turf as the top layer. I do not favour working-in muck, preferring to use it or compost, later, as mulch.

Finally, the tree is tied to the support and given a rabbit-guard.

Few apples will self-pollinate and so it is essential to have two or more compatible varieties or a family tree.

Urban and suburban gardeners are more fortunate than isolated gardeners, for there are likely to be compatible varieties, within insect range. Neighbours with apples and pears have a mutual interest in successful cropping and it is a good idea to discover which cultivars surround your own site, before making final choices.

Any long flowering decorative or crab apple is a good pollen-donor for all the apples, which flower in its season. For examples: John Downie, Golden Hornet, Wintergold and M. X *aldenhamenensis* selections.

The first season is of critical importance for the rest of the tree's life and the root system will not cope with drought. Do water freely if in doubt. Container grown trees are at particular risk, especially when they continue to behave as though still in a pot… this spiralling habit is curtailed if the roots are well teased out at planting.

Training

Form

Free growing forms are for those trees, which are free standing and will be grown as one of the following:

As a **Bush**, which is the most commonly used. It is an open goblet stemming from a 2'6"-3' (0.8m-1m) trunk, or as a **Dwarf Bush** which will similar in shape but on a dwarfing stock and branching at about 1'6" (0.5m).

Half and **Full Standard** trees are simply taller **Bush** forms…

A **Half-standard** is on a 4'6" trunk and a **Full-standard** is on 6' or more (1.5 and 2m).

Standards need plenty of room. They will be on vigorous stocks and so are unsuitable for any but the large garden or field.

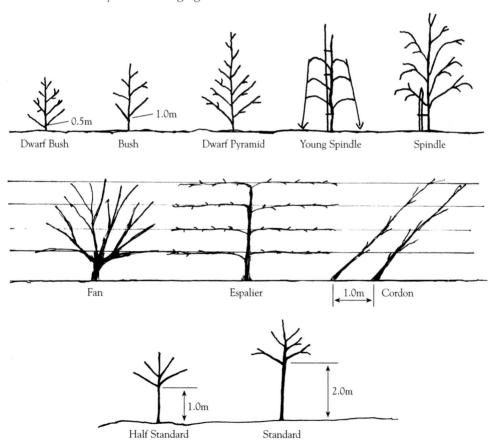

TRAINING STYLES

A **Spindlebush** has one single leader and is on a dwarfing stock. It will need a strong stake throughout its life and <u>must</u> be pruned correctly and regularly if it is to crop rewardingly.

Restricted forms

The **Cordon** is the most commonly used of these and is used against walls or wooden fences. A post and wire fence should have a number of wires, the top one being at about 6' (2m). Cordons are of great use in small gardens when the close planting (say 3' (1m)) allows greater choice and maximises access for cross-pollination.

Each cordon is planted to grow at 45°, which makes it easy to keep control of the tree's height and it increases the effective fruiting length by over a third.

Espaliers consist of a central leader with one or more pairs of permanent lateral branches and are trained on a wall or in the open on wires. A 2-tier espalier will need an about 4' (1m) wall and a 4-tier will need about 7' (2m) of wall. It was a method, much used by Victorians to edge paths or to make the walls of garden 'rooms'.

Dwarf Pyramids resemble Spindletrees but are kept lower. They are not suitable for wall training but can be post and wire trained on wires set at 1'6" and 3' (0.5 and 1m).

Fan training is very useful for apples on, for instance, a south-facing gable-end and is in essence a fan of cordons on a short trunk, which is anchored to a series of horizontal wires. Such a site encourages the ripening of such cultivars as Sturmer and Braeburn apples.

Pruning

There are a number of books, which deal solely with pruning, and it is not possible to give any other than a few pointers in this, an amateur's book. Any reader who wishes expert advice should refer to a specialist work, such as The RHS Pruning and Training Manual.

The first rule of pruning is that you ask yourself why you think that you should – and the second is to reject being bound by rigid rules, but to adapt to the needs of the time. There is no need to spend £30 on a pair of secateurs, nor can you expect much for £3… the main considerations are that the tool sits easily in the hand and that the business end is sturdy.

One system, which is useful for freestanding and larger growing cultivars, such as

Bramley's Seedling and perrypears is **to not prune**, except for the timely removal of crossing branches. The same system applies to any ornamental, crab or species tree, when there is no real need for control other than a feeling that you should. This method reduces the likelihood of useless water-wood, which often follows intemperate pruning.

I have <u>wished</u> for my trees to look like the pictures, but they do not, yet they fruit adequately. And as I age, I avoid climbing ladders whenever possible and so my simple pruning intention is to keep a tree fruiting within my natural reach.

In general, espaliers, cordons and trees on dwarfing stocks <u>**require**</u> **to be summer pruned**… To keep their growth within the space to which they have been allotted, by reducing their 'food factories' – the leaves… To allow light onto the fruit and next year's fruit buds… To allow freer air circulation and so reduce the risk of disease…and to encourage the replacement of fruiting spurs which are becoming too long. The same applies to freestanding subjects, but only if there is a **noticed need** for such control. A rule of thumb approach is to expect that free-standing trees in regular bearing will benefit from having this year's growth cut back to 2-3 buds in late July… If any earlier then there may be new growth, which will not ripen for the winter – any later and you may as well wait until winter.

Winter pruning applies more to freestanding, bush, standard and spindletrees and is to encourage next year's growth, wherever you wish it to be. **Hard** winter pruning will stimulate strong growth and is used, mostly, on young trees. **Lighter** winter pruning will be the general rule for tidying up summer pruned trees and mature trees in regular bearing. There are times when a substantial winter pruning can recover control over an ill-shaped espalier or cordon.

Tip-bearing cultivars are exempted from general methods, for with any cut off tip goes next year's harvest. All medlars, quince and some pears and apples should have whole branches removed from time to time, whilst trying to maintain the integrity of the tree's general shape. Cut back to a bud near the base of the branch to make replacement wood.

Feeding and Mulching

A tree, which has an adequate root run can look after itself to large degree, but if it is cropping regularly, then all that went into the fruit has gone away and the tree must be fed.

If in a sward, then the cut grass will return its substance to the soil, but has to borrow some nitrogen in order to break down. Young trees will not compete well with grass and weeds and the area of their spread must be kept clear. All trees should be given a dressing of muck or compost each year, sometime during the winter. I am very fortunate in having a generous winter supplier of 'grass fed 'horse' on shavings' and I apply it immediately. There has been nothing other than good effect, from its being 'fresh', but the usual advice is, that muck is rotted before use I would not use fresh muck at any other time than in winter. Surplus manure goes to the compost heap.

'Muck' and compost are, typically (0.5N, 0.5P, 0.5K), (**N**itrogen, **P**hosphorus, **K** Potassium) with varying amounts of differing trace elements. In most general terms, Nitrogen makes growth, Phosphorus makes roots and is essential in photosynthesis and Potash makes flavour.

'Chicken' is 'hot' and nitrogenous and can damage bark or kill young trees and if I had any it would go to the compost heap, where nitrogen is always useful.

'Pig' is 'cold' and needs to be opened-up with straw to oxygenating bacteria and fungi. Cow manure is hard to come by in, increasingly, arable Suffolk, but if I could source it, then it would be reserved for potting composts.

Our compost is of all biodegradable household and garden waste – fish, feather, meat, bone, hooverdust, newspaper, green prunings, weed, wood-burner ash – almost anything The heaps are rat-proofed with, expanded metal bases and covers. To the rear there is a wall. Their 4' square sides are permanent and moveable 9" x 1" planks slot at the fronts. There are three bins, the compost is turned once and we realise about three 'yard cubes' (3 x 1m^3) per year.

Even the richest of loams will be decline if it is exploited and I do not believe, that annual mulching is enough in itself and so I dress around each tree with National Growmore (7, 7, 7 NPK) annually... (If medals were struck for fertilisers then National Growmore – formulated to 'Win the War' – would receive the highest honour for long term and meritorious services to growers!). Recent research suggests that a humus rich soil is a significant global carbon sink – storing more than three times the carbon as vegetation and twice as much as the atmosphere (*Biologist* 3/2002) – and sponge for nutrients, but that it can be quickly exploited and eroded. It is the better for timely measures of inorganic fertilisers. (*New Scientist*)

I walk around each tree sprinkling at about 1oz. per yard (30g/m) and so each gets a ration according to its size. (An organic alternative is Blood, Fish and Bone (5, 5, 6.5 NPK)) – but this is to be prohibited... (BSE Foot & Mouth). I do not expect any minor mineral deficiencies, for falling leaves, mulches and cut grass replenish the stores. The most likely, if any, would be of magnesium, which is needed in larger than trace measure, being at the centre of each chlorophyll molecule. Yellowing leaves in the 'green' season would call for a dressing of Kieserite (Natural Magnesian

A very old Bramley apple tree

Limestone) and if severe and general, then a spray with Epsom salts (Magnesium sulphate) at 2oz in a 3-gallon knapsack sprayer (60g in 15 litres), sprayed to run-off.

I have the greatest respect for wholly committed 'organic' growers, but I am not one. We are as 'natural' gardeners as we feel able to be and believe that we shall pass on our land in at least as good heart as when it came to us. I feel sure that it will benefit from inorganic or organic fertilisers, fungicides or pesticides; man-made or immaculate, in appropriate measures and at needful times. I am confirmed in believing that it is man made classifications and fundamentalisms which are 'artificial' and that 'natural' is a whole, to be used and restored appropriately. I believe too, that the profligate drenching of humus-depleted soils with 'cheap' fertilisers and an indiscriminate slaughter of wildlife with cumulative poisons, is not husbandry but exploitation and will be paid for later …by all and dearly. Yet no-one is without sin!… *imported produce, whether 'organic' or not, squanders finite resources…* for example: 1 calorie of Californian lettuce costs 127 calories of fuel to get it here and fouls the environment in so doing (*New Scientist* 18.5.2002), and much of the produce offered as 'organic' does not necessarily satisfy UK 'organic' Standards.

Weed Control

If the tree is to grow in a sward then the whole area below its canopy's spread must be kept free of grass and weed for at least 3 years. A mulch will suffice, together with hand weeding but with no hoeing or tender new roots may be damaged.

Contact Herbicides

In later years when there is thicker bark, an annual kill may be made with a contact, top or totally systemic herbicide.

Paraquat/Diquat kills leaves, but not roots. **Glyphosate** ('Tumbleweed') is translocated and kills roots. Both are biodegradable, but take great care to keep spray off the tree, for both paraquat and glyphosate can penetrate young bark.

An ingestion of Paraquat will result, inevitably, in a long and painful death! Always take the recommended precautions and use a coarse spray. There are sprayer fan-nozzles available, which are especially suitable for weed-killer spraying and are sometimes supplied with the chemical. **Always** label your weed-killer sprayer clearly and never use it for any other sprays. Keep **all** poisons out of reach of children and use them according to the manufacturer's instructions.

Residual Herbicides

I use no residual herbicides. RHS Advisory Leaflet number 114/2002 lists those, which are available, but it is my opinion that there is no need for them to be used by gardeners. They can leach into waterways and aquifers and some, for examples 2, 4D and MCPA are volatile and can damage neighbouring crops.

Dichlorbenil, 'Caseron G pelleted' is used around established trees, bush and cane fruit and is particularly effective on ground elder and couch, when it is sprinkled around before any fruit-leaves appear.

2, 4D / 2, 4, 5T / MCPA…Verdone and other trade names Essentially leaf acting killers they are of great hazard to all surrounding and downwind plants in leaf, especially in warm weather, when they vaporise readily.

Orchardists use **Simazine** a residual annual-weedkiller around trees and bush and cane fruits, but many growers have given up using it because of the risk of leaching into ground water… especially through lighter soils.

Recommendation

I find that good weed control comes with annual mulching and by cutting the sward around established trees once or twice a fortnight in the season, without a grass-box. It is then necessary only to spot treat 'occasionals' with glyphosate.

Pests and Diseases

Pests

It is most probably the case with apples and pears that pests are kept within bounds without need for the gardener's intervention and that <u>inappropriate spraying damages the predator balance</u> and it is the case that plants produce insect deterrents and toxins as the growing season progresses.

Fewer and fewer insecticides become available to amateurs and the most up to date list is given in RHS Advisory Leaflet number 22/2002.

Fine, penetrating spray gives the best cover and there is little point in spraying unless the spray reaches the whole canopy.

Aphids can sometimes build up very rapidly and cause most damage in the spring, when a severe, unchecked attack can cause great loss of leaf area and even dieback. Pay close attention to the undersides of leaves for infestation. If there is noticeable damage, then a couple of commercial 'fatty acid' sprays should regain a natural balance.

Tar Oil Winterwash will dispose of overwintering aphids and eggs, but it will kill, also, fruit tree red-spidermite predators. If it must be used, then it should not be more frequently than every three years. **TOW** kills lichens, which are not only pretty, but are good indicators of a healthy environment – and so I use it only for the winter washing down of glasshouse interiors.

Apple Suckers are hardly ever a serious problem. Adults are green, with clear wings. Young suckers are dirty brown. They trail threads and drip honeydew… ants may lead you to them as they milk the honeydew. It is unlikely that an infestation will be troublesome enough to need a spray.

Capsid Bugs can be a great nuisance. They leave a corky trail as they feed on the leaves and forming fruit, which become misshapen or die. I have found that good control follows one spray of **dimethoate** given immediately after all petals have fallen. This insecticide, of relatively low mammalian toxicity, has been discontinued 'for commercial reasons' and I shall use a **bifenthrin** or some other synthetic pyrethroid when my stock has gone in 2003.

Caterpillars cause leaf damage, mainly in the spring and having overwintered in cracks in the lower trunk or in litter near to the base. We have never had need to initiate control and this – perhaps because we keep a well-stocked bird table throughout the winter? The most common and most damaging are the Winter Moth caterpillars, which can completely ruin a tree. A known problem can be reduced greatly for future years by trapping the wingless females on grease bands wrapped around the trunk in the autumn.

Codling Moth It is almost inevitable that too many apples will carry codling moth maggot right up until the time when they are bitten through, unless there has been an effective control of the moth. The very simplest and best method is to use a **pheromone trap**, which consists of a triangular plastic tube, which is re-useable, with a sticky floor insert and a capsule of female moth pheromone. It is hung in a tree in mid-May to attract and trap male moths and is effective within 50' (15m) radius… 5 trees of average size. The sticky floor lasts for about 5 weeks and is replaced by a second, which completes the protection. If the catch exceeds 15 moths per week then the problem is a serious one and there is need to, either increase the number of traps, or spray with a synthetic pyrethroid and use a grease band next autumn.

Codling moth is by far the worst fruit-pest, but the easiest to control. Trapping will suffice for the amateur, but orchardists use the traps to judge the optimum time for a minimum spraying with optimum control.

Fruit Tree Red Spider Mite, which are never red, but yellowish-brown, graze the undersides of leaves, which will brown and fall. Winter spraying with Tar Oil was the recommended control, but it kills at least as many predators as it does mites. Trees are usually in natural control, but control can be recovered may be recovered by spraying with fatty acids or a vegetable oil compound. The fungicide **Dithane 945**, which is a control for mildew, appears to be disliked by spidermite.

Pear Leaf Blister Mite is not usually of great concern, but on cultivars, which are not sulphur shy, **micronised sulphur** may give some control. It is likely that the fungicide **Dithane** discourages them, as it does red spider mite.

Pear Sawfly (Slug Worm) look like tiny slugs and feed on the upper surface of leaves. They are sensitive to the natural poison, **derris** given as dust or spray.

Sawflies in variety are at their peak during June and make their attack at petal fall. They ruin any fruit, which they enter and leave a dirty frass as they eat their way to the core. One application of derris spray or dust should regain control.

Woolly Aphid prefers to colonise cracks or damage on bark or branches and often in the crotches or at the grafting union. Not only are they unsightly but they can be very debilitating, especially for a young tree. The 'wool' is a waxy protective coat, which resists wetting. It pays to act as soon as they are noticed. Tiny colonies can be rubbed out. **Soft soap** works, but not lastingly and is best used in conjunction with a synthetic pyrethroid. Growing nasturtiums around the base of the tree is said to discourage woolly aphid. They are most visible when the tree is leafless.

<u>Recommendation</u>

The very best control for all fruit-pests is **natural control**, helped when really necessary by timely and sparing application of pesticide. <u>**Never**</u> spray whilst the flowers are open or bees are abroad.

Diseases

Fungicides which are available to the amateur are listed in RHS Advisory Leaflet number 20/2002.

Apple and Pear Scab *Venturia inaequalis/perina*. Both are fungal and ubiquitous, but specific… neither fruits are affected by the other's scab. The fungus can germinate and do damage in a very short time, particularly if the weather is warm and damp… the higher the temperature and the damper; the quicker is the damage. The result of scab is cracked and misshapen fruit and in the case of pear scab the fruit can be totally ruined. (Williams' are particularly prone). If trees have had scab in previous years, <u>then they will have it again</u>, unless a preventative programme is carried through. Four sprays should suffice to control scab...at green-bud, pink-bud, petal fall and 10-14 days later... but they will be only a part of a continuing programme against mildew. There are several proprietary brands, which are protective, and eradicant, including **Carbendazim, Mancozeb** and **Dithane**, which is my choice. **Dithane and Mancozeb** are chemically organic compounds containing the essential trace elements Manganese and Zinc. Scab inoculum can be much reduced by disposing of scabby leaves after leaf fall.

<u>WARNING:</u> **Benlate**, which was once a recommended preventative, has been shown to cause birth defects and any stock should be disposed of safely.

Brown Rot *Monilinia fructigena* is seen on fallen fruit mostly and follows bruising or skin rupture. The damage turns brown and then grows white pustules. It is spread by wasps and birds, which have visited infected fruits. The only control is through good hygiene and any damaged fruits must be cleared up and burned. Grade out bruised apples and pears from those for storing and be sure that stored fruits do not touch. See that boxes and benches are clean and freshly lined each year.

Canker has many causes but most often it is through the fungus *Nectria galligina* and is aggravated and spread by brown and other rots and woolly aphids. Poor drainage exacerbates the problem and some cultivars have no defence in even prime growing sites. (Examples: Cox, Grieve, Worcester). Some relief seems to come accidentally with the routine Mildew sprays and painting with undiluted **micronised sulphur** in the autumn has some useful effect. There are some efficacious but dangerous chemicals, which are not available to amateur growers. A recommendation, which is often given, is to cut out the canker and to paint the wound with fungicidal tree paint. My opinion is that to make extra damage is to invite further infection and I think that proprietary tree paints can hinder, rather than help, natural healing.

We have two James Grieve, which look awful, but crop reliably, and it seems to me that in wishing to grow a susceptible cultivar for its eating qualities, then you accept the problems which go along with it.

Fireblight *Erwinia amyloveora*. All pomes are subject to infection from this bacterium, but pears seem to be the most easily infected. The disease is no longer notifiable but pear trees usually die and are best destroyed. Young apple trees may be severely affected but are less susceptible as they mature. Shoots suddenly collapse and go brown and the tree takes on the appearance of having had a bonfire under it. It is much more common in the USA and amateurs are not likely to see it... I have not seen a single case. It needs very high temperatures to spread.

Honey Fungus *Armillaria spp.* All pomes are open to colonising by this fungus. The first signs are a dying back of the tree over one or more years and the later signs are the large numbers of honey coloured fruiting bodies close to and around the base. The fungus is edible but tasteless and so Honey Fungus is unrewarding for the kitchen in every respect. It is sometimes called 'bootlace fungus', for its bootlace-like mycelium, which is found beneath the bark and in the soil. These 'laces' will seek other hosts for so long as there is a food-base. There are a number of 'cures' on offer, but it is best to give in early and burn the whole of the host tree or plant. Any replacement must be of a resistant genus, for examples: beech, grasses, oak, and yew. No other fruit tree will be safe from any mycelium, which remains.

Honey Fungus is one of 'Nature's ways', for the most usual hosts are old trees and well-trimmed and virile hawthorn hedges may continue to grow healthily, whilst neighbouring pomes die.

Mildew *Podosphaera leucotricha* will happen if there is no preventative programme and is most likely to be triggered by a hot, dry spell or a rapid drying out of the soil.

'Organic' growers are permitted the use sulphur at the time of writing– for the there is no 'Organic' way to escape mildew – but many cultivars are sulphur shy, as may be any nearby gooseberries. The very best and safest control comes from extending the **Mancozeb/Dithane** scab programme with a spray every 10-14 days (according to conditions) until mid-July, followed by one after picking. They are organic in the chemical sense, but manufactured. I use **Carbendazim** from time to time to protect against a developed immunity.

Viruses are most unlikely to trouble the gardener. If any is present, then it is almost certain to have come from poor stock. It is best to buy on **EMLA** Certified Stock (**E**ast **M**alling/**L**ong **A**shton).

Physiological Problems

Bitter Pit Brown spots develop under the fruits' skins and sometimes not until during storage. It is most prevalent following hot seasons but there is no definite knowledge of the causes of this problem. Nitrogen surfeit and calcium deficiencies are cited. One 'cure', which I have never applied, is to spray the affected tree with **calcium nitrate** ('Nitrochalk') but this carries the warning that it may cause <u>excess</u> calcium and can become a further causal agent. Bramley and Egremont are particularly susceptible, but the little spots of necrosis, which are unpleasantly bitter, seldom penetrate far and usually go with the peel.

I am not convinced that the problem is of a provenancial calcium nature, but that it may be physiological and like blossom-end rot in tomatoes, its onset is influenced by sudden changes in sap pressure – following excessive or insufficient watering – when the plant prefers other nutrients to calcium and the fruit is denied its local need in the interest of the whole… But this is without scientific authority.

Cox Spot is Cox' Orange Pippin's very own Bitter Pit and may or may not occur from year to year. Again, there is little to be done, except to try and maintain good orchard practice.

<u>Recommendation</u>

The majority of pests and diseases are managed naturally or are of little or of only occasional concern. I have found that a single **dimethoate (A pyrethroid in the future)** spray after total petal fall, a **Dithane** scab/mildew programme and **Codling Moth Traps** have given adequate control over many years.

Irrigation

Large and freestanding trees are most unlikely to need watering, but it should be remembered that small trees on dwarfing stocks have less ability to find a reducing water source. The critical time is June-August when a shortage of water may ruin the crop or the tree or shock it into a biennial habit. If there is need to water then water the soil and <u>not the foliage</u>.

Thinning

Some cultivars, for example Sunset, can set far more apples than they can ripen and should be thinned if they have not fallen naturally during the **June drop** (which often occurs in July!). If the tree is then carrying an excess of fruit the **King Fruit**, which is at the centre of the cluster, should be the one, which is left if it is healthy. Naturally, strong growing trees will manage bigger crops and are left with more fruit – say two or even three per cluster.

Harvest

'Fruit', said Marshall in 1796, *'does not quit the tree until it be filled with its full compliment of nourishment'*. And certainly most cyderapples and perrypears may be, safely, harvested from the ground. Bruised fruit will not keep, but windfalls indicate that a cultivar's time approaches… Lift and twist a fruit gently in the palm of the hand… If it comes away easily at the suture, then try others. If they do too, then begin harvesting when it is most likely that the tree will harvest over many days.

Storing

Apples There is no point in trying to store early apples – they won't! If there is a surfeit of early apples, then either juice them or make early cyder, which may be blended later.

Only sound fruit will store and the very worst store is an attic or loft where apples may bake or freeze. The optimum storage temperature is around 38°F (3°C), which needs some artificial refrigeration, but a sheltered and mouseproof shed will be good enough – an average of say 45°F (8°C) will suffice. Our apples share a mouseproofed store with potatoes, which is a 15' x 7' (5m x 2m) 'room' built inside a large shed.

Along one wall is a two-tier apple bench of 2" x 1" slats on a 3" x 1" frame. The top tier is 'kitchen sink' height. Along the floor of the facing wall is duckboarding for sacks of potatoes. The slatting is covered with a couple of layers of newspapers and the apples, which have 'sweated' in buckets for a few hours, are laid on the paper without touching, stems up. They settle, naturally, to be between the slats. Each variety is kept separate and if necessary make up to three layers, each on another layer of newspaper. The consecutively harvested cultivars are arranged in seasonal order; the first to be used nearest the door and the whole crop is covered with a sheet of thin polythene, left loose. Smaller amounts of apples keep well in plastic bags; NOT sealed but folded over, which have had a pencil-sized hole per pound of fruit (2-3/kilo). When I used this method I used a paper-filing punch at 'one punch/pound' (4 holes). All stored fruit must be checked regularly for spoilage.

Cyderapples are kept in open trays under cover for the couple of weeks or so, before milling.

Pears should be stored cooler than apples (32-35°F) (0-2°C) and if there are only a few, then the best place is at the bottom of the 'fridge. We keep ours in the small cellar (which is warmer than the optimum but stable) and bring them out into a warmer room as they colour.

Perrypears are treated like cyderapples to be kept for their appropriate times before milling.

… What can your eyes desire to see, your ears to hear, your mouth to taste or your nose to smell,
that is not to be had in an orchard?…
William Lawson 17th C. Pomologist

Part of author's apple store

Apple benching

CHAPTER THREE SUMMARY

★ Apples and pears need sunshine and absence of cold winds if they are to fruit successfully.

★ A south facing wall will give 1°F/1' (1.5°C/m) of frost protection.

★ The author prefers 2-3 year old bare rooted trees planted between October and March to container grown trees.

★ Decorative and crab-apples are good pollen donors.

★ Training is either freeform or restricted.

★ Pruning should be done from necessity rather than from habit.

★ Cut sward and muck or compost are efficient providers, mulcher and weed suppressors.

★ Contact herbicides are safer than residuals.

★ Most pests are kept in check by predators, but mildews are not and require a spray programme.

★ Early varieties and bruised fruit will not store, but cyderapples and perrypears may be harvested as they drop.

CHAPTER FOUR

Cyders and Perry and Juicing and Vinegar

Real Cyder

Some Definitions: The etymology of 'cyder' is… from Middle English and Old English *sidre*… from Latin *sicera*… and pre-Christian Greek *sikera* and Hebrew *shekar*, to its root, the Sumerian *sikaru* meaning *strong drink* and so it seems reasonable to accept that, just as 'wine' began with the Sanskrit *vena*, cyder came to us, also in a westerly direction.

'Cyder' and 'cider', like 'organic' are subject to many definitions and cherry-picking. My preference is for R. K. French's… 'Cyder… a living wine of some subtlety.' And his belief that Real cyder and Real perry can come from, only, the pure juices of freshly milled and pressed apples and pears.

Some allow 'English' beer yeasts to be added but many insist that **Real** cyders and perries result only when the ferment is from the fruits' own yeasts – but more of that later.

'Cyder' was a usual spelling until sometime during the 19th Century, when it had become the usual practice for the 'lower orders' to be served, as part wages, either watered cyder – called 'beverage' – or 'ciderkin' or 'perkin', and came from the second even third pressings, called, alternatively 'small cider or perry'. Cyder of wine quality was carried on all naval ships and the ratings had daily rations of thinned 'beverage' as an antiscorbutic. When compared with the rum ration they found it thin and derided it as 'beverage' and beverage has come to be associated with soft drinks, cider, ginger beer and tea.

Her Majesty's Customs and Excise have rates of duty for Beers, Ciders, Wines, Sparkling Wines, Fortified Wines and Spirits based upon alcohol content; **Wine** being defined as containing more than 8.5% alcohol by volume – and most cyders and perries are below 8%.

So-called **Apple Wine** is made, most usually, with dessert apples and added sugar and water. It is low in tannins and acid and without 'bite' and is a wine with about 10% or more alcohol, as is the strong ale, **Barley Wine**.

Some assert that **'wine'** can come only from **'the vine'**. With the exception of Muscat, wines are described as tasting or smelling of… blackcurrant, cherry, leather, peach, ripe berry, plum, vegetal… an almost endless list, but not including grape! Cyders and perries <u>always</u> taste and smell of apple and pear.

'Fino Sherry Apple Wine' ('Progressive Winemaking' Duncan and Acton 1967) is fermented from dessert apples, bananas and grape concentrate and has around 18% alcohol content… which is about the highest level capable from any yeast.

The Campaign for Real Ale (CAMRA) has attempted to preserve the identity of **Real Cider** through its subsidiary (APPLE) – the Apple and Pear Produce Liaison Executive(!) Its **Good Cider Guide** includes sources for the two categories of Real Cider and Perry, which it allows – Categories **A** and **B**. Any cider or perry formulation, which falls outside these categories, is **Not Real**.

Category A. Only 100% freshly pressed fruit may be used and no dilution is allowed. No preservatives or colouring or added enzymes are allowed and only cider labelled <u>Medium</u> or <u>Sweet</u> may have added sweeteners 'of known safety and which must be without tastes other than sweetness'. The cider must not have been pasteurised, before or after fermentation, nor may it contain extraneous carbon dioxide.

Category B. Ciders <u>must not be made **entirely** from concentrate</u> and must not have extraneous carbon dioxide.

Whilst **Category A** is so rigorous a definition that some slight deviations are allowed – for example the addition of nitrogenous 'starter' (*Ammonium sulphate*) is allowed if the ferment is tardy, I cannot see how **Category B** does anything to *'preserve the identity of Real Cider'*. On the contrary, it would seem to invite its demise.

(Sumerian Law required that any *sikaru* maker, who cheated persistently, was to be drowned in his own drink… Nowadays one may suspect that 'quality' is no more than a vendor's notion!)

I have read that Normandy cyderists consider that English ciders are fermented from 'apple-flavoured corn syrup'. They may not be far from the mark in some cases, when the apple content can be less than 20%. The un-nationalistic truth is that makers of real cyders and perries in Britain, Germany, Spain, Switzerland <u>and</u> France are all in peril of the beverage-makers' equivalents of wine's 'Cuvée Franglais' and 'Liebfrauplonk'… But, just as there are many good factory wines, there are good factory ciders and perries, which will continue, only if they are bought in preference to poorer drinks… And it is likely, that just as the finest wines come from winemasters, then the finest cyders and perries are most likely to come from fine, independent cyderists…

It is good to drink bought cyders as well as your own. For one reason – they are our benchmarks. But do buy critically. Some 'ciders' do not include the word 'cider' or 'cyder' on the labels and so, they do not interest me. I look out for, for examples – '100% freshly crushed English (or named county) apples', or 'no concentrates used' or other indications of the qualities, which I seek.

Scrumpy used to be fermented from 'scrumps' – windfalls, and was generally cloudy from starches and pectins, drunk young and it was Rough! Hugh Stafford in A Treatise on Cyder-making (1758) reported that the variety Meadgate made *'that sort of cyder called Hewbramble, which causes a sensation as if a bramble had been thrust down the throat and suddenly snatched back again!'* It may much the same now or it can be singularly splendid cyder made from the finest of the harvest and the cyderist's triumph – or anything between. Do look out for farmhouses with 'Cider for Sale'… but go home before drinking!

In the USA cyder is known as **'Hard' cider** whilst apple juice is **'Soft' cider.**

A Brief History

Pomes of one kind have been food for Man, since the Hunter-gatherers and drink since Sumer and Akkadia. Homer (*circa* 700BC) wrote of orchards and the Romans grew cultivars… for examples 'The Must' and 'The Gourd '…and considered 'The Palernian' made excellent wine. Tacitus confirms that the British Celts used apples and pears for cyders before the Roman occupation and much poetic evidence remains of Druids' needs for pear and appletrees and mistletoe.

It was Roman practice to use legions from elsewhere in the empire to garrison their conquests and to reward long service with parcels of land… "Keltoi" legionaries from Galacia and Cantabria and Gaul continued their cyder traditions as they settled in Britain, after their military service and the Romano-British in the south-east grew, mostly, varieties for table and cooking – a practice which continues, when cyders are made, generally, without cyder cultivars.

Nordic and Germanic invaders took more than 200 years to push the British to the western fringes and most settlements with apple associations were renamed after their gods and chieftains or after geographical features. Some were given a Germanic addition… for examples Danish, Apple-(by) and Appletree-(wick) and the *'solitary appletree'* Appledore. Whether or not the newer settlers took to cyder ('wassailing suggests that they did (Old Norse *ves hael* good health), it continued in the west and the 'west' remains preferring independence and resistance to suburbanisation.

The Normans brought much improvement to cyder and perry production and introduced better cultivars. An English cyder-drinking tradition spread gradually from home centres in the east, the south and the west to become general. Eleanor introduced the culinary and perry pear Caillou from Aquitaine and the 'pie' and perrypear Warden came with Cistercian monks. By the mid-1400s cyder was used for the payment of rent or tythes, to be paid, even, in preferred varietals, such as the 'Permain wine' paid to Edward I by the Norfolk Manor of Runham each Michaelmas.

The harsh Small and Large Choke, The Wild Hedge and the Crow pears, which were uneatable uncooked, were valued as culinary or perrypears and The Gargonelle remains as one of our best, the Jargononelle.

The Pear industry was held in high regard in Tudor times and Elizabeth rewarded Worcestershire and its 'Black Worcester' pear by granting Worcester City '3 pears sable' for its coat of arms.

By the 1600s, cyder was king, but landowners and tradesmen were starting, to stretch it with water and so to sow the seeds of its decline. There were surges in popularity in times of war, when the brewing of beer declined because of its high fuel needs. Charles I is said to have preferred Worcestershire cider and perry to French wine.

Lovers of cyder continued and promoted it as 'the national home-based wine, to which the national currency should be diverted, from potentially hostile nations abroad' (Austin 1653). But when Cromwell was asked for State Aid for a National Fruit Tree Planting (Austin Treatise on Fruit-trees 1653) to... 'To supply material for joiners and for fuel; for tanners; to grow cyder rather than beer and so save fuel and grain to free the land for better use; ... and moreover Englishmen who drank health-giving cyder would be long-lived and the terror of their enemies'... He said '**No!**'

When Evelyn in Pomona (1664) spoke of 'Our design of relieving the want of wine by a succedaneum of Cider – as lately improved' he was referring to Herefordshire Redstreak. And at around the same time a London vintner won bet after bet before acknowledged judges, when he wagered that 'No Spanish or French wine can be produced (to me), which is the equal of the wine of Redstreak'.

Evelyn took small bottles of the 'Turgovian' pear perry around with him and 'many a distinguished company was astonished at its richness'... Yet, only a hundred years later Marshall in The Rural Economy of Gloucestershire (1796) was complaining of the poorness of much of that county's cider writing... 'Many would judge that it was of vinegar and water roughened with alum'... and he suggested many methods by which it could be improved.

Cyder was recognised as sovereign against scurvy and naval ships and the 18th and 19th Century Packets used to call at Falmouth to replenish their stocks of cyder and apples…

Scurvy results from Vitamin C deficiency… The teeth become loose and fall out, old fractures open, old scars dissolve, the body is covered in foul black ulcers and the breath becomes indescribably vile and the untreated sufferer dies. Cyder when *'administered to the sailor, even whose teeth are loose and he a 'dying of scurvy makes him better in two days and fitted for work after seven'*. A few years ago research into the Vitamin C content of cider found it to be around 3mg/litre and so *'Far too little to have had any antiscorbutic property'*. However, when the experiments were repeated using *Symonds 'Scrumpy Jack'* it was found to be 47mg/litre which is more than the daily need for Vitamin C… The first researchers had assumed that contemporary commercial beverage 'cider' was 'cyder'. Their pertinent 'discovery' had been how little apple it contained!

It is very difficult to assess the gravities, which were achieved by the old and gone forever, cyder varieties, but Thomas Knight, a chemist, in *Treatise on the Culture of the Apple and Pear* (1797) and *Pomona Herefordiensis* (1811) and the cyder enthusiasts Doctors. Hogg and Bull of 'The Woolhope Naturalists' Field Club', in 'The Herefordshire Pomona and The Apple and Pear as Vintage Fruits' (1886) measured the gravities of about 30 perry pears and 50 cider apple varieties. They included the last Herefordshire Redstreak in existence. The average was 45° Oechsle (5.1% Alc) with the vintage varieties having… Redstreak 79°Oe (11% Alc) Forest Styre 68°Oe (8.7% Alc) and Foxwhelp and Golden Harvey 85°Oe (12%). These gravities would have been taken after the apples had been tumped (matured in heaps) for few weeks. The relatively rudimentary equipment of the time would not produce results of the highest accuracy, but indicate remarkable juice quality. Varieties do not maintain steady gravities throughout their lives and there was evidence that Redstreak's quality had declined as the variety had become senile.

Knight enthused over the 'Teinton or Red Squash' pear for *'it affords far finer liquor than any other pear'* but went on to report that the few remaining trees were all but dead and that he had been unable to measure gravity. He raised the perry variety Holmer, which remains. The present Taynton Squash and Somerset Redstreak are newcomers and not survivors of the old varieties.

A chapter outlining improvements for cider and perry orchards and factories in the Herefordshire Pomona was written by the Reverend Charles Bulmer whose son H. P. Bulmer founded Bulmer's Cider in 1887.

It was most unfortunate that whilst Knight, Hogg and Bull and others, were campaigning for improving cyder quality and production, there were all too many who were undermining the industry.

Employers used all kinds of tricks to 'cut' the apple content and to prolong the life of already less than honest ciderkin and perkin, which partly paid their workers' wages… Boiling with spice, adding hops and mixing with 'small beer'.

And others were ruining the 'quality' market. Cyder-market middlemen agreed and fixed, ever lower prices for orchardists' crops, without consultation with them. Many made quick and effortless profit but, in the long term, they killed their goose… as is ever the case! Cyder making retreated to the farm and cottage and 'beverage ciders' drove away the connoisseurs.

It was most fortunate that some persisted in the quest for quality and after Knight, Bull and Hogg came Radcliffe-Cooke MP, and Grenvilles' founding of *The National Fruit and Cider Institute* in 1903. Radcliffe-Cooke became known as the 'Member for Cider' after persuading the government that their proposed taxing of cider and perry would gain nothing from an industry already sorely tried. His '*A Book about Cider and Perry*' (1898) covers from planting to bottle in great detail.

In 1904 a young and eager B. T. P. Barker B.Sc took over the Institute. He remained with the Institute as Professor Barker, until his retirement in 1942. The first trial orchard was planted at Long Ashton in 1903 and the Institute had trials of cider and perry trees in six counties from Monmouth to Suffolk. He was convinced that good ciders and perries came, not only from good varieties, but would reveal their different provenances and fermenting practices. He supported the orchardists and his team analysed over 2,000 juices of the varieties, which they supplied. Their findings resulted in the cyderapple and perrypear classifications, which are in use today. His scientific approach to growing and fermenting continues today at the re-named *Institute of Arable Crop Research*, Long Ashton. Sadly, and for reasons which make sense to someone, somewhere, the Institute is closing down in March 2003 after 100 years of invaluable service to growers.

H. E. Durham joined Bulmers in 1905 and was instrumental in founding their Broxwood collection with 40 perrypears and was the author of much useful research into the cultivation and fermenting of perry.

Showerings of Shepton Mallet developed a fizzy pear drink called Babycham during the 1940s, which became remarkably popular. If Babycham did nothing to enhance the reputation of Real perry, it did at least result in an increase in perrypear orchards and so a potential for better.

There is a continuing resurgence in cyder and perry drinking and this is borne out by, for instance, our local supermarket stocking twelve English cyders and ciders,

Aspall Cyderhouse Orchard

one French sparkling cyder and perry.

Western Cyder is fermented from, either a blend of cyderapples, or, in the case of special varietal cyders, from one or more 'Vintage' varieties. Its great attraction is its tannic 'bite' and cleanness.

Eastern Cyders lack the astringency of Western cyders, but whilst they may lack 'bite', they have bouquets and flavours lent by varieties, which will not thrive in the wetter west.

An exception to these generalisations is **Aspall Cyder**, which was founded by Clement Chevallier, who settled near Debenham, Suffolk in the early 1700s.

When he founded the Aspall Cyderhouse he had no knowledge of 'The Western Tradition'. He fermented his cyder from a blending of 'Norman' cyderapples, brought from Jersey and 'Suffolk' apples. Aspall cyders were fermented then, as they are now, from 100% freshly pressed and locally grown cyder, culinary and dessert fruit.

Washing apples (Aspall)

Joe 'Dusty' Miller's Mendlesham Cyder

Dusty Miller said that you couldn't make good cyder without Bramleys, which made up about ²/₃ of the bulk of his fruit and he said that 'the black ones were <u>all juice</u>'. The remaining third was *'anythin' as comes by'*. It is typically 'Suffolk' to make use what you have 'by you' and it is to be remembered that the original purpose for cyder was to preserve the apple for food and, as a drink safer than water. He used no sulphite and the apples' own yeasts fermented his cyders – he would not have used 'pure yeasts' even if he had known of them – *'Nature do it'*. The apples were crushed in an open barrel, with a washing dolly and pressed in his ancient press – (*'tul be yorn when Oi'm garn'* – but, sadly, it wasn't!). He added, as standard, a half a pound (250g) of sugar to each gallon (4.5 litres) and some free run juice was set aside, *'For me!'* He took only one pressing and sent the 'cake' for pig food. Any wasps, which landed on his horny hands were crushed under a thumb and tossed into the must'. *'Helps clear it'*. He had narrow necked 5 and 10-gallon (25 and 50 litre) carboys (ex battery acid containers) and the working cyder self cleaned by spewing over. They were kept topped to the brim with the current pressing. When quieter, the cyder went into loosely bunged barrels, previously cleansed with sulphur candles and kept full to the bung – in those days you could 'come by' barrels, quite easily! When the ferment was over the barrels were bunged down with a spigot. The cider was drinkable before Christmas and at its best from early summer. Dusty's opinion was that cyder should be still, or with a little 'prickle', and drunk at room temperature – I agree!

Dusty insisted *'He wasn't allowed to charge, 'cause o' Customs'*, but his labour was 7s/6d (37.5p) a gallon (equates with about 75p a pint now)… He knew the whereabouts of every loaned gallon-jug (*'Yur Air Force friend 's still got a jug a moine!'*) and harried for its return before next season or 'you was struck off!' His cyder was available, <u>only</u> by the gallon, straight from the barrel and was always good.

We have fondest friends who say that one of their children was 'inspired' by his cyder!

I had my own press and followed his methods then and after 'he'd gone', but without the 'black ones', which I had never really fancied – with the Bramley content reduced year on year until we found that about ¹/₃ suited our taste. The gravities, which must have been similar to his, were around 55° Oechsle, giving cyder of approximately 7% alcohol.

All went reasonably well for a year or so and then I had two successive vintages, which were undrinkable! – And, disheartened, I stopped cydermaking for a couple of years… but read a lot!

As I mentioned earlier, cyder-fundamentalists will acknowledge a drink as 'cyder' only if from its own yeasts. And there's the rub!

Microbiology

Apples host many organisms on their skins. There are the yeasts and yeast-like *Aurobacidus, Candida, Hansenula, Metschnikowia, Rhodotuleras*, and others, but few or none of the *Saccharomyces cerevisae varieties*, which are found on grapes. There are also *Acetobacter*, many other acid resistant spoilage bacteria and some beneficial malo-lactic bacteria including, *Lactobacillus collinoides* and *Leuconostocus mesenteroides*. The organisms will be of different genera and species according to the season and the time of picking and whether the apples came from the tree or the ground, but the biggest influence on the population comes from the build up of resting colonies on the cyder-making equipment. Fermentation kills off some yeasts when the alcohol content reaches 2%, some may live after it reaches 8% and some pure yeasts can just about tolerate 18%. Each yeast produces specific antibiotics, which kill competitor species and so there will be, always, a dominant flora in a must… hopefully the one you wish! Spoilage bacteria will become dominant in a weak ferment and the cider, spoiled.

Dusty's tub, dolly, press and fermentation equipment were washed with soap and hot water, which moved only the visible dirt and so his flora had become reasonably constant and of very good quality over many years. His 'house yeasts' were the dominant flora in every ferment and he had no failures. His cyder was always highly praised and 'his labour' always sold out!

That my cyders failed was, mainly, through near-clinical cleanliness! I have always used commercial compound bleach or sulphite for cleaning all brewing and winemaking equipment and the probable outcome with my cyders had been two successive populations of low quality yeasts and dominant spoilage organisms. If it were your intention to be purist then a start would be to buy a 'living' real cyder and to generate sufficient starter for your needs… And then, to store some of the first ferment's yeasts at the bottom of your refrigerator – but whether that is 'permitted' by purists, I know not.

My Cyders

Anyone with a serious desire to make cyder must do so in his or her own fashion. That which follows is 'how I do it' – and should not be read as if written in stone…

With the exceptions of the few 'vintage' varieties – and sometimes <u>even</u> then – cyders are best made with at least two cultivars, say a culinary and a dessert variety and the more varieties, the better.

A rule of thumb is 1:1:1, sour:sour-sweet:sweet, but it is best to find your own liking by trial. For examples: A selection of blends from over the past 20 years or so, which have been pleasant enough to repeat…

Worcester; Bramley; John Downie; Williams. 4:2:2:1

Bramley; Worcester. 1:2

Bramley; Lane's Prince Albert; Fortune; Russet; Cox. 1:1:1:1:1

John Downie; Worcester; Bramley. 4:3:2

Bramley; LPA; Worcester; Williams. 1:1:1:1

John Downie; Crab; Worcester, Bramley. 3:1:1:1 and…

Yarlington Mill; Dabinett; Oldfield. 4:2:1

Over the last five years friends have brought me apples in different quantities and variety and they have had, in return, cyder blended from the more than 25 varieties.

A most important part of cyder making is to a keep record of blends, gravities and methods. Another is to attempt to keep a line of similarly constructed vintages, which are tinkered with for improvement… I try something new (for me) each year, but never more than a five-gallon trial.

Fermentation… Apples

After Harvesting

Apples should be left to sweat and to mature for two to four weeks, to reach their optimum gravity and to tenderise the skins… Most of the flavour enhancing *terpenes* are in and just below the skin and we want them to run with the juice. One noble lord of old believed that the flesh of the apple was nothing but a dilutant and he had his cyder made from **only** skins and cores… no doubt, he had a compliant work force! Badly bruised fruit and 'brown rot' should be graded out. These 'black ones' may fall apart with juiciness but will pass on the rot to any touching fruit. They contain chemicals including. *2-5-diketogluconic acid*, which interferes with sulphur dioxide's abilities to bond with acetaldehyde and to inhibit spoilage infections.

Pulp

Apples and pears <u>must</u> be pulped, for they are far too hard to press unmilled.

A scratcher is the best tool for other than small quantities. A DIY Scratcher

A DIY Scratcher

similar to my own (modified from Dart and Smith *Woodwork for Winemakers*) is, essentially a 3$^{1/2}$" diameter hardwood cylinder on a spindle, with eight rows of stainless studs within a 4" x 6" x $^{3/4}$" outdoor grade ply tube. (I used $^{3/4}$" lengths of silver-steel rod superglued $^{1/2}$" deep. Alternatives include cheesehead or countersunk stainless steel screws.) The apples are pressed onto the rotated cylinder. My own cylinder is from four pieces of iroko 6" long, glued to allow a sliding fit onto a 1" square spindle which is drilled through to take a threaded spindle. allowing easy dismantling) The spindle has $^{1/2}$" thick perspex turned to fit $^{1/2}$" thick drilled perspex bearings which are fitted into the tube... Pressure is applied by a lever anchored to and above the tube and transferred to the apples by a section of 4" plastic pipe cut to sliding fit the tube and connected by rod to the lever. It has been arranged to fit onto the same frame as my grape-mill (*Successful Grape Growing*). It was turned by handle but it is, (at long last!), operated by a recovered sausage-machine. It is no faster (App 60kg/hr) with the motor, but easier.

Smaller amounts, say 10kg packs (plenty for 5 litres of cyder) can be pulped in the **freezer**. Slow freezing is best, for it bursts the cells most completely.

Another way is with a **'Pulpmaster'**, which is a rotor on a long spindle, which fits the chuck of a power drill. It is best to cut the apples into quarters and to start the operation with a tiny amount of water in the bucket.

Juice extractors work, but are a pain to use and give very poor extraction with apples. If you have plenty of time then a **large grater** will do.

… Or in some way, which is similar to **'tub and dolly'**… A length of broomhandle fitted into the end of a 30cm length of 10cm square hardwood makes a substantial dolly.

It is most important that the pulp is not allowed to oxidise through continued contact with air.

If the freezing method is used then the frozen apples should be packed into deep buckets and covered with food-grade film and unfrozen quite quickly, to finish off the cell collapse, when a quick rouse will reduce them to pulp. Left in the open they will, not only oxidise, but also attract diluting condensation as they unfreeze.

I add 'Pectolase' to the pulp at the recommended dosage and leave the pulp in completely filled and sealed 25 litre buckets, for 24 hours. The addition of Pectolase is to ensure maximum juice extraction and to prevent pectin hazes. ('Clearzyme', which is new to me, will destroy pectin, starch and cellulose in fruit pulp and wine and I intend to trial it next year.)

Equipment

Pressing

The best way to part the juice from the pulp is with **A Press** (Appendix Four). Mine is 'DIY' and it is nearly 40 years old and going strong – It is built, mainly, of 4" x 2" oak, bed-iron and threaded rod and proof that it pays in the long run, to use sound materials. (Appendix). Wine clubs and Homewine shops sell or hire presses.

An ancient bus-jack screw powers my press, but if I were building another I would use a hydraulic car jack.

Small quantities can be extracted using a 'twisted sheet' or the cyder may be fermented 'on the pulp'. This can be a messy and wasteful business, because the pulp will persist in increasing in volume and wasting ferment as it does so.

If you borrow a press, then it will have, usually, a basket and pulp bag and will work well.

My preference is for using platens and similar in principle to presses, which were used before modern drum presses. (See Appendix 'DIY Press')

The bottom **platen** is routed with juice grooves. Next comes a **juice escape**.

Each 'cheese' of pulp is contained in a 2' 6" (75mm) square of plastic 75% greenhouse shading material. The square is laid across the **cheese mould** and filled evenly – especially in the corners. The cover is drawn across to cover the pulp; the mould taken off and the next platen and juice escape are placed directly above. I have found that four cheeses are as many as my press will accommodate with ease.

Pressure is applied gradually and the juices run through a plastic flour sieve to be collected in a plastic bucket. The free-run juice can be set aside for a 'premier' vintage, but I leave it with the bulk. The law of diminishing returns applies and there comes a time when you are wasting it! Some re-arrange the pulp and press again, but I do not, nor do I take the juice off any sediment before pitching the yeast.

The spent cheeses go to the compost heap. A number of 17th-19th Century writers report that 'green walnuts' will be preserved in good condition if stored layer on layer with 'spent cyder cheeses'.

The must

It is at this point that some cydermakers test acidity and make adjustment by adding chalk or malic acid. I do not, for I feel that a particular acidity comes with a particular juice and so I go along with it.

The major acid in apples is *malic acid* (apple acid), with very much smaller amounts of *chlorogenic, citric, quinic, shikimic* and other acids together with pectins, tannins and terpenes, each with some dimension to give to the finished cyder.

It is at this time that sulphite is added at a rate of 2 Campden tablets (Sodium sulphite) per gallon (5l). Sulphite <u>should</u> be added at a rate commensurate with the degree of acidity, but since I have never measured an apple-juice acidity, I have always used the same dose and without problems. One Campden tablet in a gallon results in 50 parts per million of sulphur dioxide and this lessens through time by chemical reaction and escape.

Sulphur dioxide is beneficial in a number of ways…

It kills or stuns wild yeasts and bacteria and so guarantees the dominance of an added pure culture.

It is a reducing agent and mops up free oxygen and so, promotes a 'cleaner' flavour.

It prevents the oxidation of alcohol.

It binds on to free acetaldehyde and so prevents bottle fermentation… and…

As a free sulphur dioxide, it neutralises some charged particles and so precipitates otherwise lasting suspensions.

Nothing comes for nothing and there is no doubt that in choosing to sterilise with sulphite and to use a pure culture, in order to ensure a good cyder, then you <u>may</u> have lost the 'perfect' cyder!

Young and bottled cyder

This is the time to measure the gravity. It is done with a cylinder or bulb and hydrometer or with a refractometer. The formers are not expensive but a refractometer is and of unlikely need to the small producer. The common scale is calibrated in °Oechsle (Appendix Two) Most reasonably structured apple-juices will have a gravity (Also styled S.G., Starting gravity or Opening weight) of about 55°Oe and this indicates a Specific gravity of 1055, being 55° higher than pure water. The assumption is that this higher gravity is due to dissolved sugars, most of which are fermentable to alcohol and carbon dioxide. In the case of apples, **all** of its sugars are fermentable and are around 75% fructose (fruit sugar, *laevulose*), 15% sucrose (cane sugar) and 10% glucose, (*dextrose* – whose molecule is a mirror image of fruit sugar).

A gravity of 55° Oechsle indicates there are about $1^1/_2$lbs. of natural sugars in a gallon (750g/l), which will ferment to about 7% alcohol. My feeling is that you should not 'beef up' in order to gain alcohol content or you run the risk of imbalance, but I would be looking for some better mix for next year, if the gravity were much below 50°Oe (5.8% alc).

The Starter

Some 24 hours after adding the sulphite, heat about a glassful of juice to a little below boiling 190°F (90°C) and hold it at that for a couple of minutes. Transfer to a sterilised and still hot milk bottle, plug with cotton wool and cool to about 65°F (18°C) before adding the chosen yeast. My preference is for Gervin B which is the same 'German' style wine Yeast, which I use for white wines, but any pure culture white wine yeast or bottom fermenting beer yeast will be fine. I prefer Gervin B because it gives an appley nuance to its grape wines and because, if it finds the must to be too acid for its liking, it can metabolise some of the malic acid to alcohol and carbon dioxide.

The starter should be reproducing and showing an audible prickle of carbon dioxide within 30 minutes, when it should be pitched. It is a good idea to pitch the yeast at around the same temperature as the juice so that the minimum number of yeasts are killed by any shock from sudden temperature change.

The First Ferment (Appendix Three). It is useful to ferment in a narrow necked container, such as a carboy or demijohn. When I run out of carboys I use 5 gallon (25 litres) plastic home-fermenters, tilted so that the narrow filler is slightly raised.

The carboy is filled to within an inch or so of the top and covered with 'Clingfilm', which can be removed as soon as bubbles of carbon dioxide (CO_2) are seen. As the ferment quickens it will form a protective plug of detritus in the neck and this will be extruded for a few days. The must should be kept topped up until the tumult lessens and the must is cleansed, when the carboy gets its fermentation trap and cork. There will be need to continue topping up as the must loses CO_2. The ferment will subside and eventually, appear to have stopped and within 2 or 3 weeks the spent yeasts will 'fall'. It is at this time that another quality of pure cultures shows, for they fall quickly and form firm sediment. 'Bakers' yeast' and many wild yeasts are slow to fall and form a loose precipitate, which is easily disturbed by racking.

Racking. It is essential that the cyder is taken off the lees as soon as it seems separate and stable. This is accomplished with a siphon and tube.

This is when I make my season's blend and the separate ferments are racked into 40 gallon. (135 litres) Food grade plastic barrels (ex. Sliced mango containers) and later, from them into 5 gallon pressure barrels. One racking will do for cyder and any cyders to be left unblended are racked straight into either pressure barrels or trapped containers.

There is no need to give any permanent top pressure to barrels. The only time I use pressure is in just sufficient amount to drive the tap and to blanket the cyder.

The Second Ferment. Cyder is fit to drink as soon as it is clear and maybe before that, but a second ferment will begin in the year after making when the day temperatures are over 50°F (10°C). – Around mid-March.

Some of the malic acid is fermented to the less sharp lactic acid and carbon dioxide, by the bacterium *Lactobacillus collinoides* and others. The process produces also, small amounts in varying mixture of *succinic*, *quinic* and *shikimic* acids. It is a gentle ferment and the telltale sign is when tiny prickles of carbon dioxide appear within the clear cyder, and grow as they move upwards. This ferment may last from a few days to two to three weeks or more.

This is a time of maturation and much of the scent and flavour will depend upon which acids and esters result. What is certain is that the cyder will be greatly improved. If the cyder is too dry for your palate, then use a propriety wine stabiliser (*Potassium sorbate*) to avoid fermentation and add sugar to taste... 18g/l (2^1/2-3oz/gal) is around 'medium sweet'.

There are times, when the conditions are 'just right', when some malo-lactic fermentation will happen with the first ferment but it will not be completed. Your only clue to this having happened is when the spring ferment is curtailed.

Fermentation... Pears

Pears and perry have always been treated as though varieties of apple and cyder. Some of the most praised 'cyders' have been from mixtures of apple and pear; yet the oldest of records show that pears were known to be difficult to ferment successfully unless care was taken to accommodate their varietal idiosyncrasies. But, so long as they are treated correctly, then the fermentation procedure is as for apples.

<u>Many pears are incompatible with each other</u>, because of their differing tannins and proteins and the unpredictability of their interactions. The safest approach for the home-perrymaker is to make only single variety perries when a beginner.

Pears must be left for their particular maturation time after harvest before they are milled… Too soon and they have very little taste or sugars… Too long and they will rot from the core outwards and – at best – they will go down to an unmanageable slush. *(See Chapter Three)*

They **must** be left for around 24hrs after milling to allow the precipitation of up to 4/5 of their tannins or the perry may refuse to clear. Unlike my practice with cyder, I always take the pear juice off any precipitate before fermenting.

They differ from apples in other critical ways… Some have a large, or even the largest, portion of their acids as *citric* and not *malic acid* and some have significantly more *acetaldehyde*. There are certain *lactobacilli* which can convert citric acid into vinegar (*acetic acid*), which will ruin a perry and excess acetaldehyde may require poisonous levels of sulphur dioxide to leave sufficient to cope with spoilage. I have yet to be troubled by either of these problems and it may be that Oldfield, Brandy, Hendre and Yellow Huffcap do not present them, or that I have been fortunate that my pears have lacked the 'wrong' bacterium – but I do not know.

Some commercial producers circumvent the 'vinegar' problem by inoculating with a pure culture lactobacillium.

Another critical difference is that not all of the pear's sugars are fermentable, the main higher sugar being *sorbitol*. This results in completely fermented out and apparently 'dry' perries being mildly sweet with sorbitol and with gravities of 10-20°Oe.

Perries are said to be sometimes difficult to start. It is not a problem that I have encountered using pure culture yeasts.

<u>I would not</u> make perry with dessert pears. Dessert pears are very different from culinary and perrypears and their perries can develop a most unpleasant 'pear drops' taste from higher alcohols and esters, and, being short of tannins they are flabby.

I have used small amounts of Williams in cyder to pleasant effect, but never as perry.

Pear tannins are, mostly, the very astringent leucoanthocyanins which are colloidal and can cause virtually immovable hazes, sometimes and most aggravatingly, after bottling or when chilled to serve!... A test for stability is to check that the perry remains clear when held at 4°C for 24 hours... I have not had unstable perry and I do not know how to remedy the problem apart from drinking it at a temperature higher than 4°C!

The complexity of the perrypear is the greater because there is no generality. Some have unique amino-acids, some ferment readily, some are so tardy that commercial operators routinely add thiamine and ammonium sulphate to kick start them. It is some of their great differences, which have been the reason why, throughout the ages, physicians have selected particular pears as having either an efficacious or a disastrous effect on the bowel's 'humour'!

Do not be deterred by the possible difficulties, for so long as you attend to maturation time and take the liquor off the tannins then your perry should not be any less successful than your cyder, for the first and second ferments will proceed in the same fashion.

Juicing

All apples and pears will juice – some taste better than others – see under 'Varieties'.

Clear juice is heated as quickly as possible to 190°F (90°C) and held there for 2 minutes. Vitamin C is added and the juice goes into hot sterilised bottles. It is most important not to exceed either the time or temperature – If juice is allowed to boil then the flavour is gone and it may also cloud with pectin.

I use 'Grolsch' type bottles and add one 'Boots' 500mg Vitamin C tablet before filling, to sop up any oxygen. The bottles are cooled as quickly as possible.

Cyder Vinegar

Vin aigre is dilute acetic acid and may be produced by any of some twenty *acetobacter*, when they digest alcohol in the presence of air. Spirit vinegar is made from commercial alcohol and is devoid of other than the acid's taste, but vinegar produced from ale or wine or cyder will taste of the grain or fruit.

I have never made nor have I tasted perry vinegar, but I do not doubt that it may be made.

Firstly the cyder must contain **less than 6% alcohol**.

Half fill a demijohn with the liquor and add an inoculation of 1/5th by volume of living **natural cyder vinegar**, plug with cotton wool and maintain a temperature of 75-85°F (25-30°C). After a short time the 'Mother of Vinegar' (*mycoderma aceti*) will appear as a pellicle on the surface and this must be kept unbroken.

It will take around 3 months to produce a vinegar of 4g/l acetic acid and if the vinegar is siphoned from under the pellicle with sufficient care another batch of 6% alcohol may be insinuated.

The vinegar is remarkably harsh, to begin with, but matures to show its fruit.

Season of mists and mellow fruitfulness… Close bosom-friend of the maturing Sun
(John Keats 1795-1821)

CHAPTER FOUR SUMMARY

★ 'Cyder' like 'Organic' has many definitions.

★ Homer (c.700BC) wrote of orchards and the Romans made apple and pear wines.

★ All Kelts made apple and pear 'cyders' and British Celts made 'cyders' before the Roman occupation.

★ The Normans brought improved cyder and perry cultivars and cyder and perry became tender for tythes and rent by the thirteenth century.

★ By the sixteenth century cyder was superior to and preferred to imported wines.

★ Knight and Doctors Hogg and Bull (c.1800) wrote standard works on cyder and perry and initiated improvements.

★ Cyder and perry quality degenerated through greed and acreage reduced.

★ The Long Ashton Research Institute began and Professor B. T. P. Barker and his collaborators set standards and classification for cider and perry husbandry which continue to this time.

★ Home making of cyder, perry, juices and vinegar.

APPENDIX ONE

A SELECTION OF OLD RECIPES

All of the following old to very old recipes were recorded in and are reported in, Imperial measure.

Conversion need not be precise… 1oz : 30g 8oz : 250g 1lb : 500g 2lb : 1kg 1³/4 pint : 1 litre

Cod Quebecois. Broth of 1 cup chopped celery, 1 diced onion, 1 chopped leek, 3 cups cyder, bouquet garni, fish stock (cube?) salt/pepper. Simmer 30 mins. Run through sieve or food-mill.

Add 1¹/2lbs cod in large chunks, ¹/4 cup butter and ¹/4 cup cream. Cook 15 mins. Serve with chopped parsley.

Cotignac. Core/quarter Quinces. Add same weight sugar. Just cover with water and dangle bag of cores… Simmer 7 hrs. Separate fruit into sterilised jars. Boil liquor to a set. Pour over fruit and seal.

If you have **one quince** only then – Rub off the down, chop the fruit finely, core and all, and cover with vodka. Leave for a couple of months, or more, pour off the liquid and sweeten to taste for a blissful liqueur!

Drinks. <u>Spring</u> **'Worlidge's Warmer' 17th C.** Bruise 12 juniper berries and about the same volume of root ginger in a little cyder. Strain the juice and add to a bottle of cyder. <u>Summer</u> **'Cyder-Bismark' 19th C.** Equal quantities cyder and stout served chilled. <u>Autumn</u> **'Cyder-Royal' 17th C.** To 1-pint cyder add a double brandy, sweeten to taste and dangle a bag of bruised coriander. <u>Winter</u> **'Cyder-Bishop' 19th C.** 'Incise the skin of an orange or a lemon and stick with cloves and roast (*'before the fire'*). Put small, but equal parts of cloves, mace and allspice and a little root ginger with ¹/2 pint of water and boil until half remains. Add a bottle of port and three bottles of cyder and heat **but do not boil** and then add the roasted orange or lemon and the zest and juice of a lemon. Add sugar to taste and serve hot with the 'hedgehog' floating'.

Wild Service Liqueur. Pick just as bletting begins. Put in jars to blet a soft, squidgy brown and simmer with syrup (2 water, 1 sugar), cool and fill jars to a little less than half way. Top up with gin, brandy or vodka. Close tightly. Carefully strain off the liqueur at Christmas or, better Easter. This recipe may be used with haws and sorbs.

Williams' Liqueur. Insinuate a small set and swelling fruit and its branchlet, into a narrow necked bottle and plug the end against insects with wax or tape. Make the bottle fast. When the fruit is ripe 'pick the bottled fruit' and cover it with sugar and brandy or vodka. Cork down and wait until Christmas or Easter or later.

Himmel und Erde. Stew sliced apples and potatoes with cubes of bacon, blood sausage, salt, sugar and pepper to taste, until tender. Serve with sautéed onion.

Medlar Jelly. Said by Jane Grigson to be the very best jelly to be had with game or lamb. 1/3 firm, 2/3 bletted medlars. Cover with water. Simmer until soft. Strain. Boil liquor with sugar (2 cups sugar; 2 1/2 cups liq) until set. Pack in small jars – each sufficient for one dish.

Old English Pork. 1 1/2 lb, lean pork in 1" cubes. 1 onion chopped. 1oz butter. 1 1/2oz flour. 1/2pt stock. 1/2pt cyder. 8oz peeled & cored apples, sliced. Fry pork in butter 5 mins. Add flour, fry 2 mins. Add stock and cyder, boil, stir, 1 min. Season and cook in 2 1/2pt covered dish at 375°F; 190°C (Gas Mk7), 1hr. Add apple cont. cooking 30 mins. Serve with boiled or jacket potatoes.

Princess Gagarine's Russian Sorb Jam. Soak 2lb. Sorbs in water for two days, changing water regularly. Drain and cook with fresh water until tender… Rinse with cold water. Boil a syrup of 2lbs sugar/4 pints water and add fruit. Boil until syrup thickens. Skim/cool/ put into jars. Was served, on little dishes and with glasses of clear tea, to 'gentile' ladies…

Taunton Sauce. 3/4oz butter. 3/4oz plain flour. 1/2pt cyder. 3oz Cheddar cheese. 1 dessert apple peeled-cored-grated. Salt/pepper. Melt butter in a saucepan. Add flour, cook 1min. Remove from heat and add cyder, slowly stirring. Bring to boil. Remove from heat and add cheese, stirring 'til melted. Add apple and season. Serve hot with grilled mackerel or herring or kippers.

HYDROMETER TABLE AND USE

About 47.5% of sugars are converted into alcohol, the rest becoming Carbon Dioxide, other alcohols, the growing yeast and energy.

Cyder and perry gravities are likely to range from 45-55° Oechsle and whenever possible the must is left unchaptalised. In the cases of Apple or Pear wines, the table is used thus… Say the gravity is 55°Oe and you wish the wine to start at 75°Oe. 55°Oe is equivalent to 23^1/$_2$oz of sugars **in** one gallon (810g/5l) and 75°Oe is equivalent to 35^1/$_2$oz of sugar **added** to one gallon (1110g/5l).

35^1/$_2$ – 23^1/$_4$ = 12^1/$_4$oz (300g/5l) is to be **added** to raise the must to 75°Oe. (10% alc.)

Specific Gravity	Sucrose in 1 gal	5 litres	Sucrose added to 1 gal	5 litres	Possible Alcohol	Gravity Oechsle
1.005	2^3/$_4$ oz	85g	2^3/$_4$ oz	85g		5
1.010	4^3/$_4$	150	4^3/$_4$	150	0.4	10
1.015	7	220	7^1/$_4$	225	1.2	15
1.020	9	285	9^1/$_4$	290	2.0	20
1.025	11	350	11^1/$_2$	360	2.8	25
1.030	13^1/$_4$	415	13^3/$_4$	430	3.6	30
1.035	15^1/$_2$	485	16	500	4.3	35
1.040	17^1/$_2$	550	18	560	5.1	40
1.045	19^1/$_2$	615	20^1/$_4$	630	5.8	45
1.050	21^1/$_2$	680	22^3/$_4$	710	6.5	50
1.055	23^3/$_4$	745	25^1/$_4$	785	7.2	55
1.060	25^3/$_4$	810	27^3/$_4$	865	7.9	60
1.065	27^3/$_4$	875	30^1/$_4$	945	8.6	65
1.070	30	945	33	1030	9.3	70
1.075	32	1010	35^1/$_2$	1110	10.0	75
1.080	34^1/$_2$	1075	38^1/$_2$	1200	10.6	80
1.085	36^1/$_2$	1140	41^1/$_4$	1285	11.3	85
1.090	38^1/$_2$	1205	44	1370	12.0	90
1.095	40^3/$_4$	1275	47	1465	12.7	95
1.100	42^3/$_4$	1340	49^3/$_4$	1550	13.4	100
1.105	44^3/$_4$	1405	53	1645	14.2	105
1.110	47	1475	56	1745	14.9	110
1.115	49	1540	59	1845	15.6	115
1.120	51^1/$_4$	1605	63	1965	16.3	120
1.125	53^1/$_4$	1675	67	2090	17.1	125
1.130	55^1/$_2$	1740	71	2215	17.8	130

FERMENTATION PROCESS... MUCH SIMPLIFIED

Saccharomyces cerevisae var. ellipsoideus strains produce some half-dozen enzymes to drive the twenty or more chemical reaction chains and loops to digest certain sugars. About 50% of the sugar is used for growth and reproduction and the rest is excreted as alcohol and carbon dioxide. As the yeasts die they lend some flavours to the ferment, but if left for too long their enzymes digest them to produce off flavours and spoil the ferment.

1. Added 12-carbon sucrose is inverted to 6-carbon sugars fructose and glucose.

2. 6-carbon sugars are converted by enzymes to 3-carbon triose sugars.

3. 3-carbon sugars are digested to glycergic acid and...

    ... an end product ....**Glycerine**

4. Glycergic acid is changed   ... to...**Pyruvic Acid**

5. Pyruvic acid is digested by an enzyme and becomes

    ... an end product ....**Carbon Dioxide**

    or...**Acetaldehyde**

6. Acetaldehyde   ... becomes...........................**Glycergic Acid**

7. Glycergic acid, is either unchanged and loops to 4 or produces

    ... the end products...............**Succinic Acid**

    ... and...................................**Ethyl Alcohol**

Succinic Acid is a principal acid in the formation of aroma and taste ester.

DIY PRESS

Press Frame. T-Iron sufficient for two 23" square frames. Welded and 4 coats Hammerite. Screwed to underside of underplate.

Screw old bus jack with 10" traverse.

Arm Angle Iron and pipe 4 coats Hammerite.

Screw collar and plate bolted under upper frame.

Base. All 4" x 2" oak 1/2" coach bolted or 1/2" threaded rodded.

Feet 19" two off.

Legs 16" two off.

Inner crosspieces 12" two off.

Pressplate supports 19" two off.

Underplate 18" x 12" x 3/4" ply screwed to

Pressplate 18" square 3/4" ply two off glued together.

Pressplate sides 17" x 2 1/2" x 1" hardwood four off, glued and screwed to pressplate. Pressplate drilled to take 3/4" **Exit Pipe.**

Loose Base Platen 1 x 12" square 3/4" outdoor grade ply routed 1/4" deep with several parallel juice grooves.

Platens 4 x 12" square 3/4" outdoor grade ply. **Juice escapes** 4 x 12" square 1/2" plastic fencing. **Cheese mould** 4 x 11" x 1" battening made into a 12" open square.

All wood and metal in contact with fruit to be either finished with four coats Yacht varnish (wood) or Hammerite (metal).

BIBLIOGRAPHY

Arbury J. & Pinhey S.	Pears	Wells & Winter	1997
Browning F.	The Apple	Penguin	1998
Copas L.	A Somerset Pomona	Dovecote Press	2001
Dart C. J. & Smith D. A.	Woodwork for Winemakers	Standard Press	1977
Duncan P. & Acton B.	Progressive Winemaking	Amateur Winemaker	1967
Evans I. H. (Revisor)	Brewer's Dictionary	Cassell	1978
French R. K.	The History and Virtues of Cyder	Robert Hale	1982
Graves R.	The Greek Myths	Penguin	1955
Grigson J.	Fruit Book	Penguin	1982
Harding M.	The Green Man	Aurum Press	1999
Hayward V. H. (Editor)	Flowering Plants of the World	OUP	1978
Luckwill L. C. & Pollard A.	Perry Pears	U. of Bristol	1963
Mabey R.	Food for Free	Collins	1970
Masefield G. B. et al	The Oxford Book of Food Plants	OUP	1969
Morgan J. & Richards A.	The Book of Apples	Ebury Press	1993
Pijpers D. et al.	The Complete Book of Fruit	Admiral	1985
R.H.S.	Fruit Past and Present	K.P.C. Group	1995
Sandars N. K.	The Epic of Gilgamesh	Penguin	1960
Sanders R.	The English Apple	Phaidon	1988
Simmons A. F.	Growing Unusual Fruit	David & Charles	1972

Simon A. L.	English Wines and Cordials	Gramol Publications	1946
Tayleur W. H. T.	Home Brewing and Winemaking	Penguin	1973
Taylor H. V.	The Apples of England	Crosby Lockwood	1948
Turner B. & Roycroft R.	The Winemaker's Encyclopaedia	Faber & Faber	1979
Twiss S.	Apples: A Social History	National Trust	1999
Wells H. G.	A Short History of the World	Pelican	1956
Williams R. R. (Editor)	Cider and Juice Apples	U. of Bristol Press	?
Wilson C.	The Country House Kitchen Garden	Sutton Publishing	1998
Wilson R.	The Hedgerow Book	David & Charles	1979

SUPPLIES

Apple and Pear Trees

Blackmoor Estate, Blackmoor, Liss Petersfield, Hants. GU33 6BF
Tel: 01420 473576

Brogdale Horticultural Trust, Brogdale Road, Faversham, Kent ME13 8XZ
Tel: 01795 535286

Deacons Nursery, Godshill, Ventnor, Isle of Wight PO38 3HW
Tel: 01983 840750

Keepers, Gallants Court, East Farleigh, Maidstone, Kent ME15 0LE
Tel: 01622 726465

Marshall's, Wisbech, Cambs. PE13 2BR
Tel: 01945 466711

Frank Matthews, Berrington Court, Tenbury Wells WR15 9TH
Tel: 01584 810214

RHS Enterprises, Wisley, Surrey GU23 1QB
Tel: 01483 211113

R. V. Roger Ltd., Pickering, North Yorkshire YO18 7HG
Tel: 01751 472226

Scotts Nurseries, Merriot, Somerset
Tel: 01460 72306

Thornhayes Nursery, Dulford, Cullompton, Devon EX15 2DF
Tel: 01884 266746

Equipment

Harts Homebrews, 20 Bury Street, Stowmarket, Suffolk.

Homebrews, 10 Alexander Road, Farnborough, Hants. GU14 6DA

Homebrew and Wine Centre, 35 Crouch Street, Colchester, Essex

Luton Winemakers' Stores, 125 Park Street, Luton LU1 3HG

Microcide Sprayers, Shepherds Grove, Stanton, Suffolk

Vigo Supplies, Station Road, Hemyock, Devon EX15 3SE

Cydermakers' Associations

The National Association of Cidermakers, 6 Catherine Street, London WC2
Tel: 0171 836 2460

The SouthWest Cidermakers' Association,
Marsh Barton Farm, Clyst Street, George, Exeter EX3 0QH
Tel: 01392 876658

The Three Counties Cider and Perry Association,
Glebe Farm, Aylton, Ledbury, Herefordshire HR8 2RQ
Tel: 01531 670518

INDICES

LIST OF ILLUSTRATIONS IN COLOUR

LIST OF LINE DRAWINGS